CHALLENGES
IN THE
CLASSROOM

ELIZABETH SCOTT CARROLL

Fulton Books, Inc.
Meadville, PA

Published by Fulton Books 2021

ISBN 978-1-64654-745-6 (paperback)
ISBN 978-1-64654-746-3 (digital)

Printed in the United States of America

BIO

I was born and raised in a small town in Scotland Neck, North Carolina. I am the youngest of six sisters and three brothers. I attended Mary's Chapel Elementary School located in a small community in the south from grades K through 6.

After graduating from elementary school, I attended Brawley Middle and High School, which was also in Scotland Neck, North Carolina.

After graduating high school, I went to New York and began looked for a job, and I got a position at Chase Manhattan Bank on Wall Street and became a mailing clerk, which required me to answer phones, sort stock sheets, and send mail to my clients.

Three years later, I met and married Otis O. Carroll, who was born and raised in Roanoke Rapids, North Carolina. I became a mom of a beautiful boy, named Otis O. Carroll Jr. I didn't return and resume my responsibilities at Chase Manhattan Bank because I became a stay-at-home mom for four years after he was born. At four years old, he was old enough to attend school. Soon after, I realized being home alone all day wasn't something I enjoyed doing. So each week daily, I would take morning walks and search for work. One day I saw a sign on a large building, a sign posted with large colorful print. On the sign it read "Ursular Day Care Help! Assistant Needed!" I decided to walk in and asked for an application for the job. It was located on Rutland Road in Brooklyn, New York. Two weeks later, the director at the day care called and asked if I was available for an interview. I got the position as a teacher assistant. The hours were great!

I worked collaboratively daily with Mr. Milton Watkins. I observed and assisted him. He mentored me well.

One day he said, "Mrs. Carroll, you have a calling/gift to teach and work with children." Of course, I hadn't given that a thought, so I didn't respond to him. Days and hours passed, and Mr. Watkins continued to encourage me to assist him more by creating small groups of five students and working with them on their level of learning daily. I spent forty-five minutes with each group. I became inspired and looked forward of doing this daily.

I thought to myself, "Why not go to college and become that teacher that is needed in the New York school system of the board of education?

One day, Mr. Watkins didn't report to work. I was the only one who assisted him daily. My boss (Mrs. Ursular) asked me to begin working and teaching the pupils because Mr. Watkins and I were preparing the students for first grade. I was challenged and a bit nervous and stressed. I looked at those innocent children with their big bright eyes staring at me, waiting and depending on me. Wow! I asked myself, "Can I really teach these children alone?" I couldn't believe that was happening to me. Well, I did the best I could, and my boss was pleased with my performance of teaching and managing the students. Next day, Mr. Watkins was a no-show again. Well, what do you think happened? I had the class alone again, and I was still little nervous. So all the staff members complimented me for a job well done at the end of the day.

When Mr. Watkins returned to work the third day, he heard so many positive opinions about me. He responded, "You must start taking at least one or two courses, Mrs. Carroll." I didn't want to hear that. But I gave some serious thought about it. A week later, I went to Medgar Evers College in

Brooklyn to speak with a counselor and was advised what to do. I started off taking three classes; one of which was a reading course. I took the classes during the evening after work so I could continue working at Rutland Day Care Center and still be a good mom to my son. I didn't have any problems with the aids and other teachers. Mr. Watkins and I were the youngest staff members there.

Mr. Watkins and I continued to work collaboratively. It was the month of November, and he stated again about continuing my education and becoming a teacher.

In the month of December, he began to stay out more and more from his job. He asked how I was adjusting with my courses. I was very much inspired in December. I decided to continue my education courses, and he smiled with such an approving look.

As time approached toward the Christmas holiday, he began to be more of a no show, due to his illness. We had no knowledge of his illness, which was leukemia.

On Christmas Eve morning, we received notification that Mr. Watkins had passed away. We were all so shocked and overwhelmed; everyone became speechless. I was standing in the classroom with my students, trying not to show my emotion in front of them. He left everyone a Christmas gift under the tree and a message of encouragement.

Everyone was still in complete shock after the Christmas break, unbelieving and having difficulty digesting what had happened.

I continued my education at Medgar Evers College. I graduated with a bachelor of science degree in general education with GPA of 3.0. The same year, in the month of September, I got my first teaching position in the NYC school system. There were many challenges in the classroom.

After teaching for several years, I decided to go back to college for my master's degree at Touro University in NYC. I graduated with a master's degree in general education with GPA of 3.6. I also received a master's degree in special education with GPA of 3.5. I continued to enjoy the teaching in the NYC public school system for thirty-plus years. I thought I was done teaching, so I was hired in Long Island schools to mentor new teachers who needed assistance with their students. Just as I faced challenges, so did the new teachers. This experience inspired me to write this book.

INTRODUCTION

This book is about the teacher's role in the classroom and the challenges he or she faces through their career. As you read this book, keep in mind that the teachers are an important figure in a child's life. The teacher's goals are to assure that the child becomes a productive citizen in life. Teachers also want the children to learn how to face their challenges in the future.

CHAPTER 1

ROLE OF A TEACHER

We know that teachers help students apply concepts—such as math, English, and science—through class instructions. We prepare effective lessons also involving the parents.

Sometimes students come to school lacking affection, encouragement, and having no positive role model in their lives. I know some days in the classroom are challenging, but be kind to them; do not dismiss them, having them think that no one cares. Treat them the way you want to be treated. The Bible states, "Do unto others as you would have them to do unto you."

A role of a teacher is not just an educator. Teachers play an important role in a child's life. We shape, mold, and improve young lives, preparing them to be able to go into the world making right choices and being a productive citizen.

Perhaps the students didn't have anyone to help them with him or her homework. The teachers have the ability to make a child feel important and comfortable, even if he or she has to face problems or challenges. You can change the way the child feels by helping the child to improve his or her weaknesses or strengths. Perhaps before the end of the day, you might assign one of your strong students to assist Johnny to complete his assigned tasks. Once the child has the gist of his assignment, he or she may be able to complete his task independently.

When students walk into the classroom having a bad day, you can be a motivator by doing something during your free time to help them. You know, we must be careful of what we say or do to our students the comments you may make around them. Words are very powerful. You never know how much of an impact your words may have on your students. When you make comments, let it be something positive to lift them up.

When teachers accept a student into their classroom, they can inspire his or her students to do great and awesome things. The students can be so inspired by their teacher until they want to be like him or her, by going to college, getting a degree, and becoming an educator. Sometimes students start developing goals and dreams for themselves at an early age.

Some teachers may see teaching as a job, but it is more than a job or career. Teachers get a huge opportunity to make a strong positive influence on a young person's life. You must remember, whatever you do in your classroom, it will always have a lasting, lifetime effect on your pupils. Educators have accepted a responsibility to nurture the students as a mother or father, making sure to educate, encourage, motivate, and give them hope for the future. Educators will instill that positive energy and drive because the children have been entrusted to us for better decisions and their future well-being.

It is important that educators should encourage their scholars when they become emotional, while they are struggling, trying to complete an assigned task by saying.

For example:

1. Try your best
2. Trust your instincts
3. Believe in yourself
4. I know you can do it

Parental involvement is a positive but major step with the parents because it is the key to success. The pupils really feel very important when he/she sees two people communicating, working together on their behalf. Positive communication between parents and teachers will help the children improve their academics, behavior, self-esteem, career awareness, communication, and support for education.

Not only that, after developing a positive relationship with the parents, they can be a great support team, especially if there is no teacher assistant available. Parents will also gain respect for teaching profession. Perhaps then, the parent might be motivated enough to become a TA or teacher and help with our struggling pupils.

CHAPTER 2

EFFECTIVE TEACHER

One quality of an effective teacher is a teacher who has an open mind to change. They express themselves clearly, and he or she will explain, model, and assess the students' understanding of the content and responses on projects.

A teacher with an open mind will accept any unexpected visitor, whether it is formal or informal, and accept constructive criticism from their administrators and colleagues. They are willing to learn and try new things. It helps you to grow and do better at their teaching. Some open-minded teachers are willing to share what they have acquired.

An effective teacher will explain her expectations of the lesson by focusing on his or her objective and the required activity within the lesson. It is important that the students understand and learn what you are teaching them. After the teacher concludes the lesson, the students will be given homework as a reinforcement of what was taught.

Next day, the students will be able to share and discuss responses of the questions, which will allow the teacher to assess the students.

Educators must always teach and model expectations for the lesson to the entire class. While modeling, there must be clarity of the lesson, so they may be able to work in small groups or independently. Effective teachers motivate and encourage active engagement to all students in learning. This will allow them to feel part of the lesson and be more involved.

Sometimes students do get bored because they do not feel that sense of belonging. You may get them involved by using movement, or perhaps you may start the class with a mental warm-up in reading and math.

While students are busy working applying the skill you've taught them, you may circulate around the classroom and assess all in small groups and independent activities.

Teachers can also create effective lessons by using data assessments, conversations among the groups, and written and oral pieces of work.

CHAPTER 3

CLASSROOM MANAGEMENT

A successful teacher should have a strong rapport with her students and be knowledgeable of the curriculum and the standards. He or she must have positive class management and effective discipline skills in order to reach all their students.

The educator may have a rewarding system, such as behavior chart, stickers, pencils with positive comments and, a points system to maintain a positive environment. Sometimes, teachers reward the class by having a pizza party, Christmas party, or take the class to see a play or go on a trip.

Teachers must be consistent with rules and routines. In order to continue effective discipline skills, teachers should reinforce positive behavior and also be consistent in their teaching and planning. He or she must always be prepared, flexible, and modify all lessons to meet the needs of the students so they can have a successful lesson.

It is important to show the students interest in their personal life by having daily conversation with them and asking, "How was your weekend?" Have students write or talk about their weekend or any other day that they wish to share. Teachers must also share their weekend by modeling first, which is a good motivation for the students. This could also be used towards gaining their trust between teachers and students.

While students entering the classroom every morning, teachers could meet and greet their students at the classroom door and teaching the students to say "good morning" every day. Empathy in the classroom can have a positive result in the classroom as well as outside in the community. It helps with the diversity of students entering our school and classroom. Empathy helps students to learn and understand each other and develop positive relationships. The more we understand and learn about each other, the stronger the community. It enhances our knowledge and strengthens our cultural background.

CHAPTER 4

SEATING ARRANGEMENT

Seating arrangement is very important in the classroom. For example, you will be able to group your students based on their abilities (Teachers may place scholars in groups of according to their test scores, observation, participation and social skills). It will help with the learning process of their social skills.

Students sitting in front of the classroom are sometimes more focused and attentive on the lesson. However, sometimes students sitting in the back of the classroom are less attentive, and the teacher must move them immediately.

Good classroom management depends on the layout of the seating arrangement. There are different ways to make use of seating display. Some ways are the L-shaped arrangement, a cluster of four or six, and a circle.

These are just a few suggestions; however, I am sure you have your own creative ideas of seating arrangements.

CHAPTER 5

SUPPORT NEW TEACHERS

According to the Bible of King James Version, in the Acts 28:1–2, it is stated that "Paul was traveling on a ship with some of his followers to an island name Malta." It was a cold and rainy day. They had a shipwreck on this island, and they knew no one. When the natives arrived, they were kind; they welcomed them by building a fire so they could get warm.

In comparison, when new teachers enter a school for the first time, they sometimes feel alone, out of place, and must make an adjustment to their surroundings. As colleagues, our responsibility is to make them welcome and feel comfortable by introducing ourselves and giving assistance whenever needed. We should reach out to them, which will make their transition much easier.

It costs you nothing to be kind and cooperative with each other, so we can all have a successful and productive school year! We must reach out to each other daily. As time goes by, we are hopeful that each new teacher will feel as though they are a member of the staff.

CHAPTER 6

TRANSITIONS TO MIDDLE AND HIGH SCHOOL

Transitions to middle school and high school can be very difficult and challenging for students and teachers. It can be an experience and a growing of independence for the students. Many of the students fear these changes. One of the challenges in the classroom can be the size of the classroom, and too many students can be overwhelming. The challenges in middle school and high schools are much different from that of elementary schools. For example, teachers have to deal with excessive absentees, lacking academic, bullying each other, fighting, disrespectfulness, cursing, drugs, and weapons.

Due to lack of academic, these students face many negative obstacles. Many entering middle school and high school lack a strong background in phonic and literacy. Teachers in middle school and high school should be knowledgeable to teach or reinforce skills taught in elementary grades.

In order to decrease many of these negative challenges and struggles that teachers are experiencing in the classroom, there should be more support programs and qualified staff to help the students make progress. This can be done by small groupings, one-on-ones, tutorial programs, and the use of computer technology.

Some of the students will do better using magazines articles or news articles with a little humor. These articles are very educational and motivating.

Some of these articles are about life on earth, the American Revolution, or world history. Lesson plans are included for the teachers. There are *Time* magazines, KidsDiscover.com, *Upfront*, Scholastic. com. These materials and plans can be used by the teachers and support staff to better enhance our students' learning ability.

Career Day is also another way to expose students and motivate them to think about choosing a profession and developing goals for themselves.

Sometimes our pupils make wrong choices when they try to impress their peers. They want to be a part of or accepted, which causes them to take that path. Some of these children live in abusive homes because they lack attention and family relationships.

Sometimes the system plays a role in our children being disrespectful or rude. For example, there was a young man in middle school who was acting inappropriately daily. When the student got to school, he refused to attend his classes. While other students were attending classes, he decided to run with his shoes off up and down through the hall, screaming and disturbing the entire middle school. Of course, security and administrators escorted him to the main office with the guidance counselor and psychologists. I must remind you, this was not a student who could not do the work. This student's grades were on grade level along with the other bright peers/students. The parents were informed, and they attended the conference. The student was suspended for three days with his schoolwork packaged for those days.

The parents' feelings were hurt, disappointed, and embarrassed, as he claimed that his mother hit or beat him. The boy was so angry at his mother, he took her to court, and the judge advised the student to call him if his mother put her hands on him again. If she put her hands on him again, he would "lock her up." The child was standing, listening to what the judge said to his mother. The student was then placed in a self-contained classroom along with the special-needs students, and of course, he was pleading to be removed. This student's behavior had not improved; however, he did not leave the classroom anymore, due to the number of support staff in the classroom.

Absenteeism influences the children to get into trouble and causes them to become illiterate. They sometimes make the wrong choices, such as burglary, joining gangs, smoking, and drinking alcoholic beverages.

Many schools have classes to teach young men a trade where they can think about specific careers and be successful. Many schools have programs for girls, such as cosmetology, cooking, and sewing classes.

Teenage pregnancy is a huge challenge for teachers and students. Sometimes they want something of their own, someone to love them back. However, they haven't considered the responsibilities involved. There are struggles due to a lack of financial situations. This is why all children should value education to avoid struggling in life.

CHAPTER 7

SHARING KNOWLEDGE

Teachers, colleagues, I know your challenges and stress. I have been a teacher for thirty-plus years. Teaching is my passion.

I know there are many challenges in the school system. Some of these challenges are beyond our control, such as the classroom size, poverty, bullying, student attitudes, academic behaviors, parental involvement, and family factors.

Teachers, I want to share some of my spiritual knowledge, which I have acquired over time. First of all, I know your challenges are stressful and very difficult. At the end of the day, sometimes it leaves you with the feeling of helplessness, wanting to quit and never look back. I am sure many of you have felt and said those things to yourself or to each other. You know, often we may feel that we can do things on our own, but not true.

Since my Bible study, midnight prayer, and morning devotion, I have learned and understood about the word of God. If we all put the Lord first, he will direct our path, and the challenges in the classroom will become less and less. I cover myself with the word of the Lord every morning. Put God First! "Acknowledge the Lord in all thy ways and he will direct your path." If you do those things, your challenges in the classroom will become less and less. You will be able to walk in your classroom with peacefulness, and where there is peacefulness, there is calmness. Where there is calmness, there is learning. What I am saying, you as teachers, we all set the tone in our classroom so that every child is successful.

We are educators but we are known as Teacher, Mrs.——, or Mr.—— to the students. Our goal is to make sure every child receives a quality education and become productive citizens in society. This is how one can achieve your goal in the classroom daily. Before leaving home in the morning, you must prepare setting the tone within yourself by having morning devotion with the Lord, which will instill confidence, positive self-esteem, and a spirit of peacefulness and calmness.

When entering your classroom, your students will feel a sense of empowerment and recognize the positive energy. Your morning devotion will empower you with the energy so that you will be able to defeat your challenges in a less stressful way, because there is always a solution to your problem. "Acknowledge the Lord in all thy ways and he will direct your path" (Proverbs 3:5).

When entering my classroom, I feel the inner peace, calmness, boldness, and that positive energy within my spirit. I have determination that I will accomplish my goal to educate my students.

CHAPTER 8

MY FIRST YEAR OF TEACHING

My first challenge was in a third-grade class in the public school. My challenge was to teach two groups. I had no support. The principal said, "I do not know how to tell you nor show you how to do this, but it is mandatory as of today. All school teachers must start grouping their students by creating two groups." I had thirty students in the third grade at that time. It was my first time teaching ever. I was so scared, nervous, and stressed! I said, "Lord, I need some help here, because I don't know what to do. Lord, please help me?"

During my lunch hour, I began to think and strategize how to do this with thirty students. The only way I thought was to place fifteen students in each group. That seems easy, perhaps to you. However, that was really not the easy part; actually, there was nothing easy about it. I had to think about classroom management. Well, we know if we can't manage the class, we can't teach the children effectively. I thought an effective lesson planning for the students was required.

First, we must identify the learning objectives, design appropriate learning activities, and develop strategies for all students.

That was some challenge for a new teacher and no support. Each group was given different activities. I taught a small group of fifteen students by instructing them to move to the front of the classroom on the rug, preparing themselves for an instructional reading lesson; while the other group of fifteen was sitting at their desks, working independently and doing their best to complete their center activities.

Twenty-five minutes later, it was necessary to switch, waiting for the previous group to clear the center tables.

Two days later, the principal visited my classroom; she began checking my lesson plans, observing the lesson and my classroom management.

About a month later, members from the board of education visited my school and classroom. Let me remind you that I was so scared, nervous, and shaking all over. My legs were wobbly; my voice and hands were shaking. I couldn't hardly wait for them to leave. They reviewed my lesson plan book, observed the class and the lessons and asked the students questions about the lesson. As they responded to the questions, I watched nervously, and I wanted immediate feedback from my administrator. Everyone was very pleased of the outcome.

The first challenge was difficult, and I survived. I didn't realize or recognize that there was another challenge staring at me, until later. There was a girl in my class named Rosa. Rosa would always make sure to sit directly in front of the classroom near my desk. I concluded that Rosa was a lip reader, which made it difficult for anyone to recognize that she had a hearing impairment disability. She completed all tasks that were given but was unable to respond verbally.

One morning, Rosa arrived at school late, and someone was sitting in her chair. Little Mike was so busy helping another student complete his task. Rosa walked towards Mike, and she began pulling at Mike's sweater sleeve until he fell on the floor. He was on the floor with such a shocked look of expression on his face and embarrassment, he gracefully picked himself up and started towards me. I immediately walked over to Rosa and politely ushered her away from her group, to the other side of the classroom, because it was so out of character for her to act that way. I did most of the talking; she listened, and she motioned her head or nodded in such a way to let me know she understood everything I said. She had such an apologetic look in her eyes with so much understanding.

It was nearly my prep time, so I went to the office and requested Rosa's records. While reading her records, I discovered that she was hearing impaired. The parents were aware because she was prescribed hearing aids, but her parents could not afford to purchase them.

I went to the guidance counselor with the student's records. The principal was invited to attend the meeting with Rosa's parents and guidance counselor to decide how to handle the situation. The parents didn't know who to see or what to do about Rosa's hearing impairment. The counselor made contact with public services about the situation. Rosa was absent from school for two weeks. She was being tested again by public service doctors.

One morning, Rosa returned to school smiling, wearing her hearing aids, and she could hear and was able to participate in class discussions. She thanked me, and her parents sent me a card of appreciation and support. Rosa was a very happy child; she socialized with her peers, enjoyed working with them in small groups, and she no longer felt insecure with her peers.

CHAPTER 9

THREE YEARS LATER

Three years later I had to face another challenge. It was a challenge of thirty-two gifted and talented students in the third grade. Wow! *What a challenge*, I thought. For example, one of my students excelled in math, reading, and science. That student was always on point, with correct answers and three grades above level. However, the other students were able to answer these questions, which created a discussion among the group. They were the type of students to challenge the teacher with questions and expected an answer at that very moment. Yes, I always had an acceptable answer to their questions. I was prepared for them. When giving them an assignment, they listened for instructions and completed assignments quickly but correctly. It was as though they were having a contest. I knew then my lesson plans must be prepared more rigorously for them. Majority of the students were two and three grades above grade level. That group was very thirsty and hungry for knowledge.

Even though the students were excellent in their academics, they displayed inappropriate behaviors when they completed their task by calling out loud, "I am finished!" Sometimes they may say, "I am bored." Getting out of their seat without permission was definite a no-no, and at times I would assign them to help other (peers) with their assignments, but not give answers. They began to act as though they were teaching each other. I knew I had to review class rules. Also, I used technology to continue enhancing their learning ability and have them complete their research projects. Additional to that, I placed meaningful math and reading activities in the reading and math center, for students who complete the science projects and tasks. I must remind you, activities were always meaningful and lesson plans related.

Gifted children are wonderful in many ways. They have characteristics that could affect their social and emotional development. My students were like little professors or lawyers.

Four months later in the school year, I began to enjoy my class more and more while teaching and learning with them.

Their activities were well-thought-out, appropriately complex, challenging, and meaningful. If gifted students are not provided with appropriate learning activities addressing to their abilities and not meeting the needs of the students, they will begin to act out. So, teachers, make sure you prepare effective lesson plans.

I assess often, prepare short pre-assessments by giving the students a few math and reading questions. Just to check their knowledge level. I developed a relationship with the parents and involved them by inviting them on trips and choosing a day to visit their child's classroom. Parents can be great partners to work with.

CHAPTER 10

SECOND-GRADE CHALLENGES

After being in the third grade for a few years, my principal asked me to move to the second grade. Of course, I said yes. I didn't have that much of a choice, especially if you want your job. That school year came a little too fast for me. I was excited to take a break from the third grade. I learned that we all have challenges in the classroom, no matter what grade we might have. I had quite a few challenges in the second grade. For example, there were so many students on different reading levels. Still no support in the classroom. After reading the data, I had to start with five groups, including activities. I asked myself, "What type of machine am I going to be this year?"

Each group must have center activities on their levels. After reading instructions every morning, students are instructed to complete assigned tasks at their center table. All work was differentiated for the students, which was reflected in my lesson plan daily. Math was also differentiated instructions for the students, including center activities. The daily routine never changed because consistency was, and still is, very important for the students. Some students' math and reading levels were average and some others were far below grade level, so I worked with some of them one-on-one, while the average-grade-level students were more independent. Then others were assigned to partners after completing his or her task. That was another challenge I faced in the second grade, with twenty-nine students on my roster and still no support staff.

Almost every day, my students attended school. The principal knocked on my door and said, "Mrs. Carroll, I have a student for you." I must remind you that I still had the twenty-nine students. I nearly had a screaming fit. The students and I made HyKeem feel welcome to our class. HyKeem came the very first day without materials. A note and a supply list was sent home to his mother.

At the end of the day, I asked to see HyKeem's records from his previous school. The secretary had not received his records, so we decided to give the secretary a few more days before calling again. Well, two days passed, no records. The secretary was very busy; she didn't get the chance to call the school. When I was on my break, I called the school. A few days later, the records were delivered by a messenger.

I sat and read all documents, including his IEP (individual educational planning). I was eager to know his reading level so I could make plans and include him in my lesson. While reading the data on the student, I discovered he was on kindergarten reading level. As I continued to read his records, I learned also that he had a learning disability and a behavior problem. He had been diagnosed having ADHD. He was a wanderer and a runner. Well, I thought, I needed some help again. Weeks went by, still no help, and no one had said anything about getting me any support. HyKeem didn't know how to hold a pencil; he didn't know his letters and sounds. Of course, he didn't know how to write.

When he attempted to write or complete any task, it seemed as though he was stressed and began making strange noises or sounds that you would hear in a horror ghost movie. That definitely interrupted the learning in my classroom. Of course, I would ask him to lower his voice with the sounds. Instead of him lowering his voice, he got that much louder. He then burst out and said, "I can't do this!" He asked someone to help him with his tracing of letters and his name. He would always destroy his materials by breaking his pencil and ripping his paper. Suddenly he would run to the closet where students hung their book bags and coats. He continued making the strange sounds such as "Whooooo! Whoooo! Whoooo!" or "Huuuu! Huuuu!" The sounds were very frightening and disturbing to most of the students.

The security and the guidance counselor immediately came to my class and removed HyKeem from the classroom. I continued with my teaching and writing anecdotals about his behavior, so he could get the proper support for learning. His parents were called in on a meeting about his behavior and learning disability.

HyKeem's behavior continued to the point when he would leave the classroom without permission and sat outside in the hall at the door near the classroom. I feared that he might leave the building and into the streets. Still no TA (teacher assistant) support. I continued to work with him one-on-one. His mom started picking him up about noon time, because he couldn't handle staying in one setting for a full day. I made sure that HyKeem would receive a homework package. His parents purchased a phonics game and program to help their child. It was very challenging to the entire class, including me. His parents were a great support team. I continued writing anecdotals, so he may be placed in the right setting.

HyKeem needed to be placed in a smaller setting with students of the same disability. Finally, some months later, before school closed for the summer, HyKeem was accepted in a smaller setting with other students having same or similar disability. We prepared a pizza party for HyKeem the day before he left our school. I was hoping for him to have a smooth transition. Some of the students gave him lots of gifts, and he left with a big smile on his face.

CHAPTER 11

DAVID'S LEARNING DISABILITY

David was a second-grade student with a learning disability. His reading level was much lower than the rest of the pupils. He had difficulties with middle and ending sounds in phonics. He struggled very hard trying to make progress in his studies. As he struggled, he became frustrated, angry, and violent and began ripping paper from his notebook.

During lunch time, the children teased him, calling him "crybaby." I spoke to the students about their inappropriate behavior, and they promised not to say those mean words to David again. Many days passed, and the students continued to tease David on the bus. One evening, David's mother called the school, complaining to the principal about pupils teasing and calling David inappropriate names. His mom was very upset, because she didn't send him to school for anyone to tease and bully him. The principal assured her she would inform me about the situation on the bus. I discussed with the children about their inappropriate behavior. Of course, I used the point system to reward my students, so the entire class lost points because they were all on the bus with David, and no one would tell me who the pupils were actually engaging in bullying him.

Then all the students began to write apology letters to David. I began working with David one-on-one daily, which helped him but not enough to bring his grades up to the level needed. It was suggested that he attend after school for additional support. Mom immediately signed the papers to consent for him to attend. I was his schoolteacher, and I knew what his weaknesses were and understood what to do in order to get him to the next level.

David began making progress three weeks later. His scores continued increasing, and it became much easier for him to participate in classroom activities. One morning, the class applauded when David answered a question correctly. That put a smile on his face, and it gave him more confidence. David excelled in his studies.

CHAPTER 12

MY BIPOLAR STUDENT

Colleagues, have you ever had a bipolar student in your classroom? Well, a bipolar student is a child/student who is a huge challenge in the classroom. They are sneaky, liars, users, and they will take materials from other students. They are wanderers and runners. Bipolar students are not all-night sleepers. While you are sleeping, they are up and about thinking or doing mischief, such as watching late shows/movies or playing with his or her favorite game while parents are sleeping. It seems or appears as though they are wired up, energized most of the time. My student James was all of the above. He did not follow or obey the school rules or class rules.

One day, it all started when James took one of the students' pencil while the child was doing his classwork.

Brandon said, "Mrs. Carroll, James snatched my pencil out of my hand."

James yelled, "Stop lying, boy! I didn't take your pencil, this pencil in my hand belongs to me. Stop lying, you crybaby! Just look at you, looking so stupid!" James threw the pencil at Brandon, and yelled, "Take this pencil, stupid. I can buy lots of pencils."

I walked over to James and escorted him to his seat. I whispered in his ear and asked, "Don't you think you owe Brandon an apology?"

"Well, I didn't do anything wrong to apologize for, Mrs. Carroll. That's not fair," said James. "Brandon," James said, "I am going to let you use the pencil, all right!"

"James," I said, "you must complete your assignment now."

"Okay, Mrs. Carroll," he said. James reached in his desk and pulled out his pencil and began his class assignment.

I could never take my eyes off my students, especially James. I always circulated around my classroom every five or ten minutes with my grade book and stickers, making sure everyone is on task. The students who are always on task, they get stickers, pencils with positive comments. For example, pencils with comments such as "Good job! Bravo! Fantastic!" or a check mark.

James continued working, sitting at his desk, trying to complete his task. With a loud burst, James asked, "Am I going to get a sticker too, Mrs. Carroll?"

"Of course, James," I responded, "you will receive a sticker also, when you complete your task."

James raised his hand, and I walked over to his desk, and he whispered, "I forgot to take my medicine today."

I looked at him and thought to myself, *Oh my God!*

He said, "You can't reach my mom because she is at work right now."

I called his mom anyway, and she was at home. Mom apologized, and in fifteen minutes, Mom was at the school with James's medicine. They didn't live very far from school, so she removed him from the classroom and administered James's meds. When he returned to class, he said, "I thought my mom was working today."

I know I have named some of the symptoms of a bipolar behavior; however, bipolar symptoms are more powerful than what I have shared with you. His mood swings affects his sleep during the night and sometimes he doesn't think very clearly of what he is doing at that time. His condition causes him to have an aggressive behavior and he becomes very dramatic and uses his loud voice when he speaks.

There are times James have mood swings. For example, he would sit in the classroom very calm and attempt to do his class assignment. In a matter of minutes, he would throw his book on the floor and begin yelling, "I am not doing this and you can't make me!" He began to get up from his seat, pacing around the classroom, and glaring at his peers.

After James didn't get any attention, he returned to his seat, placed his head on the desk, and remained silent.

Sometimes a bipolar child turns to anger and rage, sometimes manifesting into violence, possibly attacking people. Bipolar students usually are not able to control their outburst. Sometimes, some emotions can turn into rage and can last for a while. If you have any student diagnosed in your classroom with bipolar, you must be patient, understanding, and kind with that child. It is important to have a teacher assistant to help with that student. A calm and patient spirit is necessary. The parents are great support staff, who should develop a relationship with families. Again, I say, always have midnight prayer and morning devotion with the Lord every day.

One way of knowing if you have a student with such behavior is to observe your students. It is important for the teacher to read his or her pupils' records and check for an IEP, if they have one.

James had such mood swings; it was sometimes overwhelming to the entire class. My support team were his parents, security, and guidance counselor whenever needed.

After teaching the morning lesson, which was reading, James began working diligently, the same as the other students. All of sudden, James stood up from his desk, walked out of the classroom without permission, and burst out loud, "I am going to the bathroom, okay, Mrs. Carroll," he said. James really didn't go to the bathroom! He began running up and down the stairs, through the hall, back and forth, ripping teachers' bulletin board papers from the wall. There were lots and lots of papers with children's work on the floor strolled down the hall. When he saw the security, he began running up and down the stairs back and forth, laughing for a while and singing, "You can't catch me! You can't catch me!" The security continued chasing him, trying to make sure he didn't run outside into the streets. It seemed as though the more they chased him, the faster he would continue to run and sing his made-up song. Everyone seemed to have gotten tired of chasing James. Soon after, the guidance counselor caught James and took him to his office, and he remained there until his parents picked him up.

The remainder of the week was very quiet because James didn't return to school until the next week.

On that Monday morning, James walked into the classroom late, with no book bag, and walked towards my desk with a note from his mom and his psychiatrist. James was calm and quiet. He completed all class assignments on time every day. Twice weekly, he was scheduled to visit his psychiatrist.

Two weeks passed, and James started inappropriate behavior. He began to blurt out loud again, "It is too quiet in here, and I am bored!" It was nearly dismissal time, and students were packing their book bags, preparing to leave soon. The matron on the bus always looked out for James, so he could have a smooth dismissal. Some way, somehow, James got off the bus and ran up and down the street, waving at the security and the matron. He continued to wave and run as though he wanted them to chase him. I have no idea how he managed to get pass the matron. He ran into the drug store near the school, hid from everyone, including the principal. He was in the drug store sitting in the back, on the floor in a corner. His doctor prescribed a stronger medication for him; however, it lasted until three thirty or perhaps until four o'clock.

I returned into the building to make a phone call to his parents so they would know the reason why he was going to be late getting home. The driver of the bus eventually left the school. James and the other students arrived home safely.

I thought about the danger and challenges everyone faced, inside and out of the school. I decided to plan, strategize, to give James some responsibilities. Working with a partner daily, the teacher and principal monitor was what he needed. Sometimes he was a line leader. Finally, a teacher assistant was assigned to be with him daily, everywhere he occupied space. I used this to improve his behavior, eliminate conflict, and create a safer environment. As you can see, some challenges requires multiple strategies for one child.

CHAPTER 13

INCLUSION CLASS

About every year, the board of education makes decision to add new inclusions to the class on every grade.

Well, I was told by my principal that she wanted me to teach kindergarten inclusion class with Mrs. Mathis. The classroom was huge. Mrs. Mathis was a very nice and cooperative teacher to work with. She was originally from Russia. We looked around in that classroom, and we realized the work needed to be done, including decorations. We had two weeks to get the room ready and prepare for our parents' visit.

You know, if we were not ready on the first day of school, the teachers would be graded if the rooms were not prepared, and believe me, you wouldn't want that to happen. One day, my principal said, "A wise man is always prepared." If you know the truth, I made sure I was always prepared.

Mrs. Mathis and I worked very diligently together. During the first day of school, we were all very busy. For example, that very same day, parents wanted to meet with the teachers and see their child's classroom, admiring the beautiful decor. After, the parents visited the classrooms and would speak with the teachers, but they were unable to do so at that time. They decided to walk their children to his or her class. Everything was going well until I heard a child crying and screaming while walking through the halls, coming directly towards my classroom. I was hoping that wasn't my student. Guess what? That was my student. I thought to myself, "She has first-day jitters." Her mom stayed with her for about an hour until she calmed down. Wow! That was a relief for everyone in the classroom and the school.

Soon after her mom left, Jasmine got out of her seat and sat on the floor in her pretty clothes. I did ask Jasmine to return to her seat so all of us could get acquainted with each other. Jasmine continued to sit on the floor, and she refused to move.

"Jasmine," I said, "let me show you how to write your name? My name is Mrs. Carroll. Can you write your name?" Jasmine started crying and screaming again. At least I got her to sit on her chair.

I went to the next student, and he began writing his letters (ABC). When the student finished his letters, he said, "I can write my name too, see!"

"Johnny," said Jasmine, and she watched him. Jasmine looked at me and asked, "Help me write my name too?"

Jasmine was all right, I thought, until someone touched her name on her desk!

"Stop! Stop! Leave me alone," she said. "Mrs. Carroll, Johnny touched my name on my desk. Please tell him to stop."

"Johnny," I said, "didn't Jasmine ask you to stop? What are you supposed to have done?" I asked.

Johnny said, "Move my hands."

"Please let Jasmine have her personal space?"

Everything went well the remainder of the day.

Our next day was all right until Jasmine walked into the classroom with her mother. Her mother walked her to her seat, helped her unpack her book bag. Then her mother turned to leave the classroom, and Jasmine began to scream, saying, "Mommy, please don't go, come back because I want to go home!" Jasmine threw herself on the floor, began rolling her body like a ball, kicking and screaming! Her mom had tears in her eyes but continued to walk towards the door and out of the classroom because she had to go to work. When her mom closed the door, Jasmine chased down the hall after her mom. Security saw her running. She stopped her, scooped her up, and returned her to the classroom. Jasmine continued screaming, and I began writing anecdotals, documenting her behavior. I decided to start keeping my classroom door closed because I had a screamer and a runner. What a challenge she was, so I made a point to have her sitting next to me daily.

For six months, Jasmine performed every morning, kicking and rolling on the floor. Soon she calmed down, but still there was no support. Jasmine needed an assistant to be with her daily. I decided to introduce her to a phonic program, making good use of technology. The program, Starfall.Com, was recently installed for helping pupils such as Jasmine. She enjoyed the program. She learned her letters and sounds and was able to match words with pictures. She learned to write her name and simple words such as *like, how, I, cat, me, my*, and *she*. I used my award system such as stickers, big bucks, stars, and check marks for all students when earned, especially when they are completing their tasks. You know, Jasmine became one of the students doing very well in her studies. She was one of the principal's monitors and line leader. What a relief for everyone. Jasmine was a very happy and cooperative child.

CHAPTER 14

SEVERAL YEARS LATER

Guess what? Another four years later, my principal asked me if I would pilot another inclusion class. I opened my mouth and forgot it was open. I asked, "How do you want me to do that?"

The principal's response was "You figure it out, you did it before." She said, "You are the general ed teacher, and Mrs. Davis is the special ed teacher."

Fear and stress came over me, and I had to sit down.

I must say, teaching an inclusion class does not always work out. The two people must be compatible in order for it to work effectively. An inclusion class consists of 60 percent general education and 40 percent special education. There were twenty-five students in the classroom. We sat down immediately, began reading data, other documents, discussing our plans for seating arrangements, analyzing and planning effective lessons, and differentiate instructions for all students. I thought to myself, *What another challenging year*. Inclusion was mandated by the board again, and they wanted us to start piloting the class immediately. I began feeling as though I was being used as the guinea pig, as some people may call it. Then I said to myself, "Why me?"

The principal gave us about a week left to prepare and get everything together. We had to set up the classroom, lesson-plan, decorate the classroom for second-grade inclusion class, and read the data on each student, because data allowed the teacher to understand students' weaknesses and strengths. This was used as a guide to plan, teach, and address the needs of the students daily. Also, it helped with effective planning. Teaching inclusion students can be very challenging because sharing a classroom with another teacher is like a marriage.

Compatibility is very important. Or it will not work because there are differences of opinion. It is okay to disagree or agree. For example, I remember when Mrs. Davis wanted to complete an art project doing reading instructions; however, I suggested that it would not be such a good idea because anyone could walk in at any time unannounced, including the board members.

Mrs. Davis thought about what I said, and she agreed with me. There were two students in our class and they were diagnosed having ADD. The students' names were Joseph and David, and they were the two most needed students in that class. They needed supervision every day.

Joseph had a speech disability. When he was unable to repeat a word, he began cursing and banging on the desk. He developed such anger; sometimes he would punch Anthony, which seemed to be for no reason. Mrs. Davis would always take him out for a walk until he calmed down. Sometimes she had to take him to the guidance counselor for a time-out period.

Joseph's negative behavior caused for multiple anecdotals to be written daily. The staff contributed to Joseph's success. Joseph began to make progress in his studies with the help of his teachers, guidance counselor, speech therapist, and parents daily. Due to the support, Joseph continued to work very hard in his studies. As a form of assessment, Joseph was able to use the computer to enhance his reading ability.

David was my other student with a reading disability. He had to have one-on-one support services due to his low reading level: K. I made sure

David was paired with one of my independent and compassionate reading students.

Mrs. Davis and I would always take turns in working with David, while other students continued working on their activities in their groups. I made sure all pupils were on task by circulating the classroom with my assessment folder. When circulating the classroom, it allowed me to assess their understanding while they are conversing with each other. When circulating your classroom, use that strategy for classroom management. We continued using our reward system, which would enhance our classroom managements. The reading coach often pulled David out of the classroom into a smaller setting so she could assist him with his studies.

At the end of the week, the monitors for each group will tally their scores. If the groups get at least two-third of the stickers or check marks, at the end of the week or end of the month, the students will make a healthy fruit snack. We choose some of our favorite fruits (grapes, strawberries, or bananas). Teachers, make sure your students do not have food allergies before trying this and get permission from your administrators.

CHAPTER 15

DARNELL WITH "ADHD"

Darnell was one of my fifth-grade students. He was diagnosed with ADHD. He had a learning disability, and he also had difficulty staying in his seat for long periods of time. His attention span was very short. In the midst of his lesson, he would begin standing, stretching, walking back and forth and around as though he was at home, perhaps forgetting the setting he was in. When I reminded him to return to his seat, his response was, "Oh! Oh! Okay, Mrs. Carroll." If I didn't watch him very closely, he would disturb the other students by knocking their pencils from their hand and pulling the girls' hair. Sometimes he would walk out the classroom without permission. Trying to sit in the classroom during an entire lesson was very difficult for him. My lesson was always differentiated for students with same disability. However, the challenges I faced in the classroom became more advanced and more adult-like. I created many anecdotals, meetings with guidance counselor, parents, and SBST for solutions. Some days, the psychiatrist visited and observed his behavior, academics, and participation in the classroom. Still no support teacher.

One day, there was a situation when he left school and went to Manhattan on the train alone. Little did I know that Darnell had received a small package from a suspicious made-up friend. Some of the students saw him accepting a small package from a male adult. When he came to class, he put his book bag into the closet like the other students.

After breakfast, the morning lesson had started, and everyone was very much engaged in the lesson and activity while Darnell claimed he had an urgent need to use the bathroom facilities. Teachers always permit the students to go when they ask. Students are assigned with a partner because they are not allowed to go alone. Immediately Darnell disappeared from school, ran past security through the doors, and ran into the street to the train station. When he reached Manhattan, New York, later, he was seen walking as though he was looking for an address, and when he found it, he went into a building. The policeman watched and waited until he came out of the building. He noticed something unusual about him, a child with no book bag, a fifth grader alone on a school day unsupervised. The officer stopped him and questioned him. Darnell was unable to answer the officer's questions, but he did give him the name of his school, so the officer called the school and his parents in Brooklyn. His parents went to the precinct and picked him up. He was not on medication at that time because they were trying not to have medication prescribed for him; however the doctor had discussed that idea to his parents so Darnell could function in the classroom like the other children.

Finally, his parents took him back to the doctor, and he prescribed something to help him focus better on his school activities.

Two weeks passed, and I noticed how Darnell was more relaxed. A member of the family would walk him to school every morning for safety reasons. Darnell's academics began improving, and he was assigned to work with a partner daily, and his attention remained focus on his studies. His classmates always encouraged him to complete his task by working with him daily. Darnell worked cooperatively with his teacher and peers. At the end of the second quarter of the school year, his grades began to improve.

CHAPTER 16

GIFTED AND TALENTED PUPILS

After teaching the gifted and talented class in the third grade, I didn't expect or planned to teach them the following school year. However, the principal's plans were totally different.

At the end of the school year, she requested that I looped with the gifted students to the fourth grade because majority of the class were girls. To be exact in the count of students, there were twenty-two girls and ten boys in my class. Well, I thought to myself it would not be too much of a challenge because I knew them and their behavior. Educators should carefully plan his or her lessons rigorously, meaningful and interesting. Each lesson should end with some form of a follow up or an assessment. It will help students to remain focus on lesson taught and will enhance a positive, effective classroom management.

There were other challenges I had to face that I did not think of them. Two months later, I was given another student. Her name was Tasha, and she was also an excellent student in all subject areas, including her drama class. She was given a lead part in a Christmas play, and she learned her part and performed well.

During rehearsal one day, the problem began. When rehearsal was over, they were dismissed and returned to class. The drama teacher was having a difficult time trying to return them to their classroom. I heard loud voices coming from the students. They were complaining, "That's not fair, I was here before she was," "I should have gotten that part," "Mrs. Hewitt just like her better than she like us," and "I don't want to be in the play anymore." Another replied, "I don't want to be in the ole stupid play either." There were so much dialogue between them, I had to meet the class and walk them back to the classroom.

Since the conflict spilled over into my classroom, I decided to defuse the situation by talking to my students about their inappropriate behavior and what they could have been doing to avoid the conflict. After discussing how awful they sounded, they apologized, and the girls became friends once again, I thought. I noticed some of the girls were still having a little jealousy between them. I was very disappointed in their behaviors because they were so disrespectful toward Mrs. Hewitt. I encouraged each student to apologize to Mrs. Hewitt. They decided to write her apology letters.

I began monitoring and recording their inappropriate behavior daily. Everything was quiet for a while, and I noticed that some of the girls were writing notes and passing them to Tasha. She began crying, while her head on the desk, because the girls threatened not to be her friend, and they didn't like her because she tried to be too cute on the stage. The girls allowed jealousy to get in the way of friendship.

One day, Tasha didn't want to come to school, so her mother sent me a note and asked me to talk to her. Immediately I informed the guidance counselor and the drama teacher. We created a small group meeting, discussing the situation with the involved students and having them to share their feelings. The students were encouraged to apologize once again. In and out of the classroom, the girls continued to be nice to Tasha.

However, the groups always competed while completing the task. They enjoyed having dialogue, discussing questions and answers. As time passed, they grew to really like Tasha, and they all became very good friends, by sharing lunch, things they did on weekends, classwork, and studying together. Guess what? One of the students had a sleepover, and the four girls included Tasha. They went together, and all had a blast!

CHAPTER 17

ALEX'S STRUGGLES

Alex was a third-grade student and seemed to have some type of learning problem; however, his symptoms didn't seem to be like some others I have had. Alex appeared to be hyper, inattentive, and violent. He had a difficult time sitting for a long period of time, trying to complete his assigned task. His reading grade level was level 1, and math was level 2, but yet, he was in the third grade. I met with Alex's mother, and she was aware of his violent behavior, and she had an appointment for Alex to visit a doctor, hoping to get some type of support for her child. Alex was very challenging in the classroom, and I was forever writing anecdotals for his mom to take to his doctor.

Whenever I asked him to complete his classwork, he would complain about not being able to do it, but he would never try. Sometimes he would burst out loud, "I don't know how to do this!" Volunteers offered their support, but he refused every time. He responded, "Leave me alone, I can do this myself." But really, he couldn't do it, so he continued the struggle. I worked with Alex one-on-one so he could complete his task. Other pupils worked independently in their groups; Alex was more relaxed when I worked with him. He was too ashamed to work in groups with the other students. I believed Alex would do much better in a smaller setting or an environment where he could get more support. He was very destructive. The more he struggled, the more frustrated he became while writing. Sometimes he destroyed his supplies—break his pencils, rip his work, and throw it on the floor. I encouraged him to clean up the debris on the floor.

One day during gym, Alex became very angry and violent. He hit one of the windows with his fist. As a result, the window cracked, and pieces of the glass fell on the floor. He was asked why did he do such a thing. His response, "I was angry!" Blood was dripping everywhere from his hand, on the floor. Immediately, he was taken to the nurse for medical attention. He was then taken to the emergency room to get stitches because it continued dripping blood profusely everywhere.

However, his inappropriate behavior did not improve. He walked out of the classroom one day without permission, which raised a red flag of concern. I began to think about the risk and danger involved, so I called for security for support. Chasing after him was definitely a no-no due to responsibilities for the other students. After Alex was evaluated, he was placed in a smaller setting to get the extra support that he needed to make progress in his studies. He began to read independently, solve math problems, explain the answers, and became willing to help those students who were having difficulties. Now Alex came to school with such confidence, with a smile on his face, ready to learn. He loved to read animal and car books, and he also loved history. His grades improved tremendously.

CHAPTER 18

SHY AND WITHDRAWN

Anthony was a very quiet student in the third grade. He was diagnosed with ADD. ADD is known as "attention deficit disorder." His reading level was on grade level, and math was on first grade level.

He never responded or participated in class discussions. When Anthony was asked questions, he would always stare at you and not respond at all. This behavior continued whenever anyone attempted to talk to him. At one point, I thought he could not hear or talk, so I went to the guidance counselor and discussed Anthony's behavior.

That behavior continued for almost three months. Writing anecdotals was extra work for me, but I was concerned and wanted to help Anthony. We reviewed his files, called his mother, and invited her to attend a conference meeting with the guidance counselor and teacher. His mother came in the next day, and she explained, Anthony was a very active child at home, and she didn't have any problems with him talking or playing at home with his sister and brother. He was in school every day, still no change in his behavior.

One day I decided to encourage Anthony to sit near my desk, one-on-one, so I could help him with his activities. He did as I requested. He was having difficulty with initial letters and sounds, so each day, I worked with him. I discovered that he was too shy and withdrawn to work in small groups with the other students because he could not keep up.

He had a lack of confidence. I knew I had to get him through his insecurities, so I continued working with him and encouraging him daily by assisting him with prompt answers to his questions in order to strengthen his shy soft voice. He started repeating his initial letters and sounds orally. He started writing words with meaning and complete sentences. Anthony received rewards daily (stickers, pencils), and he became a happy child in the classroom.

Soon after, I assigned him to a partner, in a small group to continue helping him in his academics. His confidence and academic continued to improve daily.

One day I heard Anthony say, "Stop! Stop taking my paper. You ripped my paper!" I walked towards the group, and Anthony went under the table and sat on the floor. I encourage him to come and talk to me. He refused to move, so I walked away, and then he came to me. His partner stopped working with him, and they began ripping each other's classwork. I began recording his inappropriate behavior because that was unacceptable. Anthony must know there were consequences for his actions by taking away points, making changes on the reward chart, contacting parents, and getting no computer time.

Anthony came to school the very next day looking a little sad. I asked him, "What was wrong?"

He replied, "I can't use my TV nor computer."

I asked, "Why can't you have your television and computer, Anthony?"

He said, "Well, because of my behavior in the classroom yesterday."

I said, "Anthony, you know we talked about this in the classroom, and you know there are consequences behind every action."

He continued looking sad and said, "I am sorry, Mrs. Carroll."

I explained to Anthony that he must wait until it is your turn. Everyone, including administrators, knew Anthony was in the wrong setting; however, I had to continue working with him until he was placed in his proper setting.

CHAPTER 19

CLASS INTER-VISITATION

Today, I pushed into a kindergarten class, and I observed the students and their behavior. Quickly, I was able to identify the challenges in the classroom. One of the challenges was with a student named Jeffery. He had a problem that had not been diagnosed at that time. However, the teacher had to stop during her lesson daily and write anecdotals about Jeffery's behavior. This was really a challenge because the teacher could not complete her lessons effectively. Each day, Jeffery stood in the middle of the classroom and screamed and screamed so loudly. The teacher tried to continue teaching her lesson, but she was unable to do so. The noise was very loud, so the assistant teacher always removed Jeffery from the setting so the teacher could teach the lesson for the other pupils. When the TA walked the child to the principal's office, she was unaware of such behavior in the classroom, so she decided to observe Jeffery's behavior. The TA is the teacher daily support staff, and sometimes I was there to be her additional support.

This teacher was a new teacher, straight from college, and needed all the support she could get.

The next challenge was a medical challenge in the classroom. This medical issue was something that the parents had not dealt with yet. I was hoping and praying that his parents would take care of it soon. The student's name was Marc, and he had serious nosebleeds. Not only was it the classroom teacher's challenge, it became my challenge also. Today was not easy for me to watch a helpless child go through that, so I was sure it wasn't easy for Marc. His nosebleed did not appear to be normal. It was running like water all over the floor uncontrollably. The child began to cry. The TA would always take him to the nurse and stay for at least one hour. The nurse would always send him back to the classroom, and about half an hour later, he returned because the blood flow had not stopped.

At the end of the day, my last challenge for the school day was making sure twenty-five students were placed on their correct bus. After speaking to the students, I realized not one of the students knew their bus route, so I used the bus route chart to help place the children on the bus. That challenge was completed with great success.

The next day, I was still concerned about Marc, so I decided to visit the classroom, but not as a support staff. I needed to talk with the teacher in charge about the student and his medical challenge we experience yesterday. The teacher was happy to know about my concern.

I was disappointed to learn that Marc had another severe nosebleed the next day. The challenge was overwhelming to everyone, including the entire class, due to the excessive amount of bleeding. It was all over the floor. The students began to cry and had to be removed from the classroom at that moment. One of the nurses immediately came to the classroom to help the child until the bleeding was under control. Parents and an assistant were called, and they arrived at the school immediately.

The class was cleaned and sanitized before the students were allowed to return to the classroom. Marc's parents took him to the hospital for additional testing and care. I was waiting to hear about the report on Marc's condition.

CHAPTER 20

VIRGINIA IN THE FIRST GRADE

Virginia was a first-grade student. She had never been inside a school or classroom in her life. She had never been inside a nursery, pre-school, or day care. Virginia didn't know how to hold a pencil correctly, which told me she did not know how to write at all. You know, I had a tremendous challenge before me.

She was eager and excited to learn her letters and sounds. I created worksheets for her name, letters, and numbers so she could trace them. Sometimes, I would go to the teacher's store and purchase some activity books on phonics, literacy, and math workbooks, so I could make copies of various activities.

Each morning, while teaching my phonic lessons—which was my foundation—and my literacy lesson, Virginia would participate like the rest of the students. She enjoyed echoing the letters and sounds with her peers. She was able to identify her letters by using the pictures, colors, and matching them next to the letters. Sometimes I made good use of technology by using the phonics program (starfall.com), which was installed and used by my independent students. This program also had a grading system so each child could be graded and monitored.

Virginia was definite academically delayed. She had not really known her letters and sounds except for the letter *V*, the first letter in her name. She could not identify her numbers except for the number 5, because that was her age. She could identify shapes, for example circle and square. Her attention span was very short.

However, she attempted to respond to the teachers' questions even though she did not know the correct answers. She wanted to be accepted by the other students and be friends with them. She was very verbal and friendly to everyone in the class. Due to her participation in class, including working one-on-one with her daily, she began to read more, participate more, and conversate with other students. When given her homework, there was little parental involvement. Her homework was not always completed. Since lacking support staff, I always worked with her one-on-one daily to help her achieve her academic goals. Eventually, I began to see improvement in Virginia's verbal skills, especially when responding to the teachers' questions. She also began to identify letters, sounds, and learning to create simple words that were previously taught. She began reading, making predictions by using easy books with pictures, and she enjoyed having book talks.

Virginia improved enough in her academic studies so she was assigned with students in small groups. The students were very encouraging and supportive. You could tell by her performance that she enjoyed being with her classmates.

The next year, Virginia went to the second grade; she was more verbal than before due to the confidence she developed within herself. She was a great monitor, line leader, and class helper. She enjoyed helping the other students who were academic delayed. It filled my heart with joy watching Virginia make progress and helping others. She focused on her assigned task and grades continued to improve daily.

CHAPTER 21

THE TWO SIBLINGS

Quasia was in the third grade and the oldest sibling in her family. Quasia needed support with her academics and socialization skills. Her phonics, literacy, and math were not on grade level. She refused to socialize with her peers in the classroom and to participate in small group activities. Every morning when she entered the classroom, she seemed to be a very unhappy child. However, she never wanted to talk to anyone, not even the guidance counselor. She was sent to the guidance office many times because we had no emergency contact number. The contact numbers we had were not working.

Their grandfather was the only one seen bringing them to school every day. He did not allow them to take the school bus with the other children. It seemed as though he was very protective of them. It also appeared to be no female role model in their household for the children.

One morning, the guidance counselor saw the grandfather dropping the children off for school, and she invited him into her office. His name was Mr. Franklin, and he was a deacon at his church. The children would always go with him to church every Sunday and Wednesday nights. Their grandfather resumed the parenting role. One morning Quasia came to school after literacy block, and all the teachers in the school had started their lesson when she walked in. She appeared not to have had much sleep the night before. She cleared her book bag and put all materials inside her desk.

"Good morning, Quasia," said the students. She did not respond.

I asked Quasia would she like to join us. She still did not respond. *Oh well*, I thought to myself, *give her some time*. The pupil had no one to help her with her homework, because her grandfather lacked understanding of her assignments. Since there were no support staff, I worked with her one-on-one during my preparation time to assure that she would improve, move forward, and make progress in her studies. Eventually, she began to get along with her peers, she became more attentive and participative in her class activities. She began maturing a great deal, becoming more happy and friendly with her peers. I monitored all students daily, assessed them once a week. This challenge was resolved a few months later when her grandfather remarried. Mrs. Franklin was a great help to Quasia and her brother. She made sure they completed their homework assignments. This experience in the household could have a negative impact on Quasia's and her brother's Self-esteem and their maturity as adults. "It could also prevent them from becoming productive citizen in society.

CHAPTER 22

MRS. SANDERS'S CHALLENGE

Mrs. Sanders was a first-grade teacher who worked at an elementary school in Brooklyn. She was very enthusiastic, energetic, and wanted nothing but the best for her students. Mrs. Sanders would always stay after school to create activities for the next day's lessons. She enjoyed every minute of her job.

One day, she had an awful day. That day seemed as though she couldn't do anything correct. First, the AP and principal walked into her classroom and asked to see her lesson plans after observing her lesson. She directed them to the desk in front of the room. The assistant principal and principal left and told her they would return her plan book. They were not supposed to take her lessons plans, she thought to herself, but she didn't say anything. Instead, she went to the chapter leader, but she wasn't any help.

She said, "They can take your plans if they discover that your lesson plans are not fully developed or incomplete. Perhaps they lacked detail information and not aligned with the standards which causes ineffective plans."

On day 2, they returned and gave back her book. She read each comment, which stated that the plans were unorganized and not related to the lesson. They also made a note saying the students were disruptive, noisy, and had poor classroom management. Mrs. Sanders was highly overwhelmed and disappointed because she planned and checked her work before presenting it to the class, because she felt the plans were fine. The administration staff discovered her lessons were not well planned and thought out or organized carefully. After reading the comments about her plans, she scheduled a meeting with the assistant principal. The meeting did not go as well as she hoped it would. As a teacher, we must always prepare detailed lesson plans aligned with standards and make sure our plans are affective. If the principal says it is not necessary to do detailed lesson plans, that's fine. Until then, your lesson plans represent you as a teacher, and if you are not sure, make sure you check with a buddy teacher or meet with one of the administrators. You must learn to help and support each other. Effective lesson planning, good positive classroom management, and a good delivery are keys to success.

CHAPTER 23

TOMMY, A SECOND GRADER

Tommy, a second grader, was given an interclass transfer because of inappropriate behavior. Whose class was he placed in? That's right, mine! I remember when the teacher across the hall told me I was getting one of her students. *Why me?* I thought to myself. Anyway, Tommy arrived, and I assigned him a seat in the front of the room. He sat quietly for a minute, looking around at his new surroundings.

The next day, I met his father, who informed me that Tommy was suspended from his previous school. He punched the teacher in the face, and she refused to press charges. So Tommy was transferred to my school and my class! He refused to do any work. He was a runner, always leaving the room without permission and running down the hall. I remember when the principal tried to talk to him, and he ran off to some place in the building. The security guard tried to find him and continued looking for him. By now, I knew him well enough to relax because he would eventually return to class.

When the guard left, Tommy returned to class with a smile on his face. I discussed the behavior with Tommy, asking him what should he have done differently.

He replied, "I don't know, I don't want to be in this stupid school. I'm sorry." He knew his behavior was inappropriate by the explanation he gave. Not only he was discussing his behavior, but he had to write about it. Tommy tried to complete the assignment, but he was having difficulty. I could tell he was a struggling student because he was unable to spell some of the basic sight words. He had missing letters and incorrect spellings. Tommy was so frustrated and overwhelmed that I assisted with organization and sight words on his paper. I realized that this child's behavior was caused because he was not on grade level, and he didn't have a well-rounded foundation. He didn't have knowledge of basics. He needed support, so we worked every day on a one-to-one basis to help him improve. He became more comfortable and eager to learn. He was getting the basics, and he wanted to learn more.

Tommy attempted to complete his assignments independently and began making progress. At times he would volunteer to explain and solve a math problem. During assembly program, Tommy received an academic certificate for improvement. From that time on, he continued to improve. He trusted me, and he was more relaxed in the classroom. He knew I wanted him to help himself become successful. His behavior changed by being more cooperative and listening attentively. He made significant progress in his studies. Good for you, Tommy! Keep it up!

CHAPTER 24

SEEKING ATTENTION

Lauren, a fourth-grade student, was someone you must keep focused on her because she would walk out the classroom without permission. She acted very mature, more adult-like. She felt as though she didn't need to ask for permission to do anything. She wore a little lipstick or a heavy-shade lip gloss every day and always entered the classroom late. She no longer wore school uniforms to school as the other children; she wore her tight jeans and sleeveless blouse.

One day I noticed she was on her phone talking and texting to someone in the classroom while the teacher was teaching. She wasn't doing any classwork and had no interest in her studies that day. I informed the teacher, and of course, we were allowed to confiscate the phone if inappropriately used, especially in the classroom. I pushed into the class that day and observed her behavior. Mrs. Taylor asked Lauren to place her phone on her desk.

She responded, "This is my phone, you didn't pay for it!"

"Well," the teacher said, "if you don't put it on my desk, I will call security, have you and the phone removed. And then, I will call your parents."

Lauren walked slowly towards the teacher's desk. She replied, "That's not fair. May I have it when I am ready to go home, please?"

"Of course not," replied Mrs. Taylor.

Lauren sat down, placed her head on the desk, and began sobbing, saying, "That's just not fair, I need my phone for this evening." When it was nearly time to go home, Lauren asked if she could have her phone again. "Please, Mrs. Taylor. May I have it now?" she asked

"No, Lauren," the teacher answered. "Tell Mom to come to school tomorrow," she said.

Lauren went home without her phone. Next day, Lauren came to school with a better attitude about her phone. The phone was given to the principal for her parents to pick up. Lauren didn't want to do that. Immediately she began to cry and scream, "Someone gave me that iPhone so I can call and text them."

One day a man came to school to pick up the phone. He thought the teacher had the phone, so she redirected him to the principal's office. At that moment, we thought that was her dad. Lauren answered, "That is not my dad, he is my friend."

"What do you mean your friend?" I asked.

"Mrs. Carroll," she said, "that is my mother's friend. My mom told me she was going to send him to pick my phone up. I have never had anyone to ask me questions the way you did, Mrs. Carroll," said Lauren.

"Well, there is always a first time to some things," I replied.

"Are you a mother, Mrs. Carroll?" she asked.

I replied, "Yes, I am."

She began watching me without conversation, looking so amazed.

The next day, when Lauren came to class, she watched me working with my group of students. She walked towards my group and stopped. She quietly pulled a chair at the table and began participating in the lesson. Lauren continued joining my reading group every day. I preferred that she sat in with my group of students than walk out of the classroom. Having her near me every day became less challenging and peaceful.

Mrs. Taylor and I agreed to have her join and sit with my group because it was absolutely less stressful.

We were very concerned about her behavior. She continued dressing like a grown-up. *Someone must talk to her about her school uniforms,* I thought.

The social worker and the guidance counselor gave additional school uniforms to add to her wardrobe. She still didn't wear them. Academically, she was one of our strongest students in all subjects. She shared correct answers to the questions when asked. She enjoyed class discussions. Lauren became a group leader and monitor in her group. She always helped others when needed.

CHAPTER 25

THE OLDEST FOURTH GRADER

Dwayne was a fourth-grade student, a holdover, and thirteen years old. He was the oldest and tallest pupil in the fourth grade. If he had done his work and passed the state test, he would not be in that situation. He should actually be in the middle school with his peers.

He was a disturbance in the elementary school classroom, and he loved bullying the other children daily. Sometimes he would put his head on his desk, go to sleep, and wake up, and the students would sometimes help him with his schoolwork. Dwayne engaged into many fights and arguments with the students. Most of the time he would do silly and inappropriate things, seeking attention. For example, walking near the girls, pulling their hair, making them cry during lunch and recess. He would tease the children about their sneakers. He was not allowed to go outside anymore to play with them during recess time. Dwayne was suspended numerous times for bullying the students and displaying other inappropriate behavior, such as running through the hall playing. He was caught by security. He asked, "Why are you taking me to the office?" He began kicking and yelling and saying, "Take your hands off me!" He yelled again, "I haven't done nothing. What are you doing?" The security continued to walk Dwayne to the principal's office.

His parents were called and asked to pick Dwayne up early from school before dismissal. He was truly a challenge in elementary school. Whenever he displayed inappropriate behavior, he always denied ever doing such things. He was always saying, "I didn't do nothing, everybody always calling me out and putting everything on me. That's not fair! I am not coming here tomorrow."

Well, would you like to know, the principal asked me to push into the classroom every day and work with Dwayne one-on-one. When he learned about me working with him, he said, "No! No! Could you all please give me someone else? Mrs. Carroll will make me work all the time. I am not coming back here anymore." Of course, the next day, he was in his class waiting for me to help him. He was so far behind, it was heartbreaking.

He struggled trying to read and sound words, but he was unable to do so. His reading level was on first-grade, and with math, he was on second-grade level. I used lots of manipulatives, foundations skills, materials, program, Starfall.com, and iRead: Reading Programs, which was installed in the computer.

Later in the school year, Dwayne began to improve in his academics, especially when he began reading simple words in his literacy book, writing sentences and creating short stories. He began volunteering answers in math and peer tutoring. His attitude began to change and became more receptive towards adults and authority. One day, he wrote a letter to his class, apologizing for his inappropriate behavior. Not only was he the oldest student in the class, but I could tell by his writing that he was not on grade level. From that moment, I made sure to continue working with Dwayne on one-to-one basis to continue progress.

CHAPTER 26

PEER INTIMIDATION

Theo was a fourth-grade student. Academically, he was on grade level. However, he had many severe problems. He was diagnosed having ADHD and supposed to be on medication. The teacher and I had to write reports and anecdotals about Theo's behavior daily. He would attempt to provoke the other students by bumping into them while walking in the hall, changing classes, and calling his classmates out of their name. He would also push them aside and make them fall. Theo had a strange behavior that the children in the classroom had a sense of distrust towards him because of his unmannerly and rude behavior. Sometimes he would ask a student, "What are you looking at me for?"

The student would reply, "I am not looking at you."

"Liar!" Theo said." He stood up, walked out of the classroom without permission and slammed the door. Security was called, and she returned Theo to class. We could hear his voice. "Get off me! I know how to walk! Put me down!" he yelled.

He would not sit in groups with other students or socialize with them in a positive way. He always sat alone in front of the classroom, near the teachers' desk. When he was not at the school, the teacher and students seemed to be more relaxed and comfortable with each other. I could tell they enjoyed the class and not have to watch and see what Theo was doing or about to do.

One day, Theo came to school later than usual. He unpacked his book bag, and something small fell from his book bag on the floor. I heard the students say very loudly, "Ooooooh! Mrs. Carroll and Mrs. Miller, I see something pointed, long and shinning."

We walked over to retrieve the object. It was shocking to both of us to see such object looking so sharp, like a scalpel. It looked like something a surgeon would use during surgery.

Immediately, I called security for assistance. They came and removed Theo and the object/weapon from the classroom. The security asked him to walk with her to the office. He began yelling, "What are you doing? I haven't done anything! I just got to school! Get your hands off me, woman!"

Theo appeared to be in the wrong setting. He belonged to a big brothers' club at school. One of the members and I were always working with him daily. If I wasn't there with Theo, a member of the club would spend more time with him in his classroom, so the teacher could teach her lesson effectively and in peace. It was a real challenge and stressful to have Theo in the classroom without support.

The parents were called to attend a conference about the object that was in Theo's book bag. The parents came to school to see the principal and the guidance counselor. Theo intended to use the object on another fourth-grade student.

The two boys had differences of opinion during a basketball game. They began accusing each other of cheating, which led into a fight. The coach broke up the fight, talked to both boys, and they apologized to each other and led everyone to believe the problem was resolved. They started back playing basketball that very same evening. Soon after being on the floor, perhaps ten minutes, Theo jumped on Amir, punching and kicking him. The coach put Theo out of the game and off the team because of his violent behavior, rudeness, disrespectfulness, and for not listening to the other coach or any other adults there. Theo always tried to solve his problem through violence. The final decision for Theo was to suspend him for three days and also given a verbal warning about homeschooling him. His parents agreed with the decision. In the meanwhile they were looking for a teacher to homeschool him. It was also suggested that Theo should attend school half days until the end of June. Since Theo had been in the middle school, I had been tracking him, wondering how he was doing and adjusting to the change. Teachers would inform me about his behavior in hoping he would change and grow up to be a successful young man.

Unfortunately today, I received some disturbing news about him and his progress. Today, I was informed that he became angry. He grabbed his teacher and began beating on her in her chest multiple times. 911 was dialed, and EMS arrived immediately and took her to the hospital. At this time, we are not sure about her condition. However, administration and parents were seeking transfer for Theo to attend alternative schooling. Everyone was trying to make sure he was placed in an appropriate setting and have a smooth transition, so he could be successful in society. This decision must be thought out very carefully to make the right choices for him.

CHAPTER 27

SHY WITH COMPLEX

Damel was a student in the second grade. He was the largest and tallest student in my classroom. He was shy, and he seemed to have a complex because of his size. However, he was very low in his academics and needed lots of support. He was the most needy and challenging student in my class. He didn't like working in smaller groups with the other students. Due to the fact that there were other students in need of my support, he wasn't very cooperative when working with them because he refused to sit in groups.

One day he was assigned to a small group and refused to sit with his friends. He replied, "I don't want to sit with them."

"Well, Damel," I asked, "why don't you give it a try? Perhaps you would like to sit with your friends."

"I rather stay in my own seat," he responded.

I developed a small group, just enough for three students, near my desk. The students were sitting in their group, so Damel began walking slowly towards my group, while looking back to see if his peers were watching him. He stood near my group, watching the other students reading and answering questions. I invited him to join us.

Finally, Damel sat down, still watching the students in my group. He began to be too busy drawing in his notebook and writing on his desk. He started making spit balls, throwing them across the classroom, hitting other students. This was shared with the principal. When she entered the classroom, she witnessed Damel throwing spit balls. She spoke to him about his inappropriate behavior and threatened to call his mother.

His mother was at work, so she said she would take care of everything when she got home. She must have spoken to Damel because when he returned to school the next day, he was more respectful and friendlier with his peers. Months later, he seemed to be maturing on his grade level, and he became more interested in his academics. His reading and math scores improved. Even so, I encouraged his mom to allow him to join the afterschool program, which was what he actually needed, so he could continue to improve in his studies. As time went by, he continued to show progress, and his self-esteem improved.

CHAPTER 28

OUTBURST

"Shut up!" Gabriel yelled across the classroom to another student.

"We don't tell anyone to shut up," responded the teacher.

"But he called me dumb just because my answer was wrong," said Gabriel.

Since there was inappropriate name-calling, the teacher decided to have circle time for conversation. This was usually done after lunch whenever there were conflicts in the lunchroom or school yard. The teachers would always allow the students to have ten minutes of circle time to resolve any conflict that might have taken place doing their lunch recess. Many teachers decided to allow the students to have this opportunity to resolve any differences they may have to avoid interruption during their teaching time.

Mrs. Jackson faced that challenge every day; however, her strategy was always successful. Gabriel was a fourth-grade student who was short in height and very verbal; he talked constantly, complaining about something every day, and he was not on grade level. He liked to read independently, so he always chose a book with pictures because the picture book helped him figure out some of the words and understand the story better. He could read a level "H" book with pictures.

Gabriel struggled with math; however, he attempted to solve simple math problems (such as 23+33, 5x30) and sometimes simple word problems. I continued working with him one-on-one, and sometimes when assigned, he worked in small groups.

A meeting was scheduled with the CSE, his teacher, his guidance counselor, and his mother. His mother suggested to place him back in the third grade; however, we were not allowed to do that. The principal disagreed with such thought because he was too old and may cause regression. Besides, he was held over in kindergarten, and the teacher informed her of some learning disability. The mother knew that her child needed extra support, and she began to cry because she didn't know what to do.

After the discussions about Gabriel's academic performance, it was suggested that Gabriel be placed in a twelve- one-on-one class or assigned to a class for one period where phonic was taught. He would also get some pull-out services. His mother agreed for him to take one period of phonic and return to class for small group instructions. Gabriel started improving in his studies, with the support of his teacher assistant; however, he must continue working to improve his behavior.

CHAPTER 29

ONE-ON-ONE

Pushing into an inclusion first grade yesterday was a very challenging and disturbing day to observe and watch a student who obviously needed some extra support. One-on-one would be helpful and appropriate for the students and teachers. This child was very low in his academic; he didn't have knowledge of phonics or his numbers. Maurice's reading and math level was on kindergarten. It was difficult for the teacher to give him what he needed to be successful without support. Mrs. Baker asked Maurice on numerous occasions to return to his seat. He responded, "In a minute, okay!" He began flipping over his head, made cartwheels on the carpet in the classroom. His inappropriate behavior could lead to a total disaster, I thought.

The principal walked into the classroom, observed the teacher's reading lesson. What a nervous wreck the teacher was. I was sitting there feeling her pain and stress, especially the way she was speaking. She did ask Maurice to join her doing the lesson. Maurice ran and hid under the computer desk. The principal sat down and began writing while the teacher continued teaching her lesson. In the meanwhile, the student was still inattentive, and the principal invited Maurice to join his group. Instead of Maurice joining the group, he decided to run under the computer table and hide. The principal was still writing and observing the teacher and the class. The principal said, "Mrs. Baker, I believe Maurice is ready to participate in the class discussion now."

The teacher walked over to Maurice and, using her quiet voice, asked him to return to his seat and join the lesson. He remained under the table. Mrs. Baker continued her teaching because she could tell other students in the class were getting restless and bored, by hearing the sighing, talking, and others beginning to tap on their desks. At that moment, I knew she was about to lose control of her class.

The principal recognized what was happening also, so she excused herself. She responded to the teacher, "I will speak to you later." And she exited from the classroom. The teacher looked relieved, but also upset because of the uncertainty of what the principal may say in her observation.

Maurice definitely needed one-on-one instructional support to assist him daily. He needed time out to walk to guidance counselor and call his parents to inform them of their son's inappropriate behavior. The team called a meeting, which included the guidance counselor, psychiatrist, parents, social worker, and principal—if she or he wasn't too busy. It was necessary for the team to strategize and plan for a safer environment for Maurice and everyone involved. The parents did agree with the decisions that were made. The mother stated her oldest son had similar problems, and he got through school all right. She really didn't want to have Maurice tested. He was unable to remain in his seat for more than fifteen minutes. He was constantly out of his seat, ready to do more cartwheels in the classroom as though he was a gymnast and walked back and forth outside the classroom unsupervised.

The teacher said, "Mrs. Carroll, he does this every day."

I replied, "That is unsafe for everyone".

Maurice needed academic support. (teacher aid) to help with his phonics, reading comprehension and math because he was far below grade level and having a difficult time achieving in those subject areas. It was suggested that he needs help from our support Staff daily because his setting must be modified for his learning.

<<insert photos here>>

CHAPTER 30

MRS. FEN

Mrs. Fen was a great teacher. She was a caring and loving teacher toward her students. She was nearly ready for retirement and had three boys in her fifth-grade class who were disrespectful. They were always displaying inappropriate behavior in the classroom by making spit balls, throwing them, hitting the girls, calling out, using foul language— and of course, that was unacceptable.

Mrs. Fen had developed some type of illness due to a lot of stress and challenges she faced in the classroom. I was assigned to her class to support her. She was very grateful for my support, and I was happy to help her. Every day I was writing anecdotals, calling parents, and walking them to the principal's office. They were always on detention, sitting out during gym time, while watching other students participate. During recess, they had lunch, returned to the classroom, and completed their classwork. I thought to myself, there must be an effective way of handling the situation. I just made suggestions and prayed that it would work.

The three boys would feed off each other, no matter whether they were indoors or outdoors. They were very tall and large in body for fifth grade, more like the size of a seventh- or eighth-grader. When I went to their class, I always separated the three boys. One of the boys always had such a scowl look on his face when he saw me coming. I could hear one of the boys trying to whisper, "Ah man, here she comes again." And the other boys sucked their teeth. I always removed two of the boys out of the classroom and taught them in small reading groups of 4-6 pupils so the teacher could teach the rest of the students effectively.

I modified their setting by taking them to a much smaller classroom so I could support them in the work the teacher prepared for them. It also gave me the opportunity to review phonics, simple words (*I, them, they, him, where, that*) and simple math to help them gain confidence in themselves and minimize the inappropriate behavior. After each academic activity, the students were given the opportunity to share their responses. This led to a whole class involvement and increase in their self-esteem. It was increased to the point of helping other students in the classroom and encouraging them to complete their tasks. These students became more independent, and less assistance was required to the point where they were able to work with their classmates. The inappropriate behavior was minimized. Everyone began making progress in the classroom.

Remember, if there is constant interruption in the class, the teachers can't teach, so there is no learning. One of the students volunteered to assist students in the afterschool program. This decision made him feel confident, and he attempted to accept many challenges that came his way. He became a proud and respectful young man.

CHAPTER 31

TARDINESS

Juan was a fourth-grade student who was very quiet and came to school late every day. If he was not late, he was absent. Juan rarely participated in class activities. You must call on him to answer. Whenever he was called, he just looked at you with an "I don't know" look, so he needed to be prompted with clues in order to answer questions. The teacher was trying to help Juan feel comfortable, but he seemed as though he didn't care.

One day, while the students were solving math problems, the teacher noticed how Juan was sitting there staring into space, not focusing. "Juan," the teacher asked, "what should you be doing?"

He responded with his mouth open, "Ah... ahhh," not knowing what to say.

The teacher ushered him to the back of the classroom and explained the directions to him again. She asked him to explain what he was asked to do. He was able to recall information given. She then assigned two of her strongest students to sit in a small group with him and encourage him to complete his tasks. Those students appeared to be her most compassionate students.

Next, she gave the students a bag of manipulatives to help solve the problems. Juan had such a difficult time solving the problems. He was confused, not able to recognize the numbers. The teacher realized that he needed support in identifying the basis addition and subtraction facts. I offered my support to help Juan. After working with Juan for a short period of time, I began to see the growth in Juan's academics. He needed support, consistent drilling and encouragement until he developed positive confidence within himself. The next week was coming very fast, and the class was due to have an assessment test. Well, Juan was trying very hard to solve his math problems. He needed lots of encouragement and positive self-confidence to make progress.

After giving the assessment to the class, the data showed improvement in Juan's performance task. Juan's improvement enabled him to be included in the middle group. However, if he continued improvement, he would be able to work with the higher level of students, in flexible grouping.

Support staff came into the classroom daily to enhance his skills. Juan no longer felt isolated from the other pupils; however, he gained positive self-esteem.

CHAPTER 32

ART CLASS

It was Friday when I observed and interviewed one of my colleagues in middle school. She was assigned to an art class. You know sometimes when you think about an art class, perhaps it may be easy; you may think and say it's just a piece of cake. You really don't know much about the challenges you will face there in the classroom. On that particular day, Mrs. Cohens thought that way, but she had a very difficult and challenging day.

One of my principals said to me one day, "A wise man is always prepared." If you prepare an effective lesson, most likely you will have an effective delivery. Three girls walked into the classroom, loud, cursing, using foul language, and having no respect at all. Mrs. Cohen asked the girls to leave the inappropriate behavior outside and dial the noise level down. Mrs. Cohen responded once again, "Young lady, please, do not speak that way in here."

The three young ladies laughed, "Hahaha." And they said, "What planet are you from?"

The teacher didn't respond to any of the comments. She continued discussing the project they were supposed to work on until completion. The three girls continued the inappropriate behavior. They appeared to be like bullies, trying to intimidate the teacher and didn't care whether she was an adult or not. Before the end of the class, the girls had thrown lots of paper, and Mrs. Cohen asked the pupils to stop throwing paper on the floor. One student responded, "You are not my mother, so you can pick it up yourself. We are not doing it!" This statement angered the teacher because they refused to do what she asked them to do. She realized that things were not going so well for her. She called security for assistance, and he took the girls to the office and told them not to leave the office until they saw the principal.

Soon after, the girls returned to the classroom to clean up the mess they made. One student whispered to another student, "You should hit her with the broom." While cleaning the classroom, they continued using foul language.

Finally, the girls finished cleaning the classroom and were ready to leave. The teacher was standing near the door.

One student attempted to push her, but the teacher was very much alert and watched the girl walk towards her, and she swiftly moved herself away from the door. The girls looked at the teacher, at each other, then sucked their teeth, rolled their eyes, and mumbled to themselves.

"Wow!" the teacher said. "I can't believe all this rudeness."

When Mrs. Cohen spoke to the security the second time about the pupils' behavior and the language they used. The security responded, "I am not concerned about the language they used." He was used to hearing that kind of talk from them.

Mrs. Cohen was upset and began walking through the hall thinking to herself, This is not for me. She left the school and was transferred to another school. She is enjoying the children at the other school doing what she loves to do. Mrs. Cohen learned to be a good motivator for her pupils and prepare an effective lesson.

CHAPTER 33

CHALLENGES

Teachers have many challenges in common. For example, Mrs. Glades was a social studies teacher, who was accused of mishandling one of her students inappropriately. She was accused of hitting her student during class. The student said the teacher was pushing her and shaking her. She went home and complained to her parents about the incident. She knew that the teacher was not allowed to put her hands on her. That gave the parents the opportunity and leverage to take the information to court. They filed a lawsuit against the teacher and the board of education without having accurate facts.

Mrs. Glades was suspended immediately from her job without pay for three years. During that time, she was placed in a room called "the rubber room." It was a room used for teachers who allegedly displayed and were accused of inappropriate behavior—for example, cursing or putting hands on pupils. The teacher was there for an unlimited amount of time, until her hearing. Due to the fact this incident never happened, so the teacher's union lawyer defended that case.

However, she was determined to win, but she lost the case on the first trial. Still no pay! The union lawyer did not give up, due to the lack of facts. The teacher's lawyer and her personal lawyer cooperatively worked together and proved her innocence—still lack of evidence. Jasmine (the child) was questioned again. She began to cry, sobbing and saying, "Mother, I am sorry, I lied. Mrs. Glades didn't touch me. I got mad at her because she wasn't going to take me on the class trip with the other children. I wasn't listening to her, instead I was talking back at her, and she asked me to stop being disrespectful."

The facts were given, and the truth was told. As the trial continued, Mrs. Glades was found innocent and given her back pay for the past three years she lost. She was given back her social studies position, and she resumed her teaching career immediately.

Another challenge Mrs. Glades had to face in the classroom were the negative thoughts of the students because of what they heard about the subject. The students were confused about the nature of social studies. Mrs. Glades loved teaching the subject, and she enjoyed and knew how to motivate her students, capture their attention, and make it fun. She encouraged the students and parents to take field trips with her, which was prepared to educate and enhance their knowledge because it was so limited. The teacher invited the parents to cook different types of foods, she shared different types of music, arts, culture, and clothing. She challenged their minds, so they may have visions, dreams, set goals for themselves and think about their future. That was a huge challenge for Mrs. Glades, so she was very selective of the topics she planned. She stayed within the guidelines of the district policy and prepared an effective lesson for a good delivery.

CHAPTER 34

HIGH SCHOOL SCIENCE CLASS

Mrs. Hartley was a high school science teacher; she was an awesome teacher. To be a science teacher, he or she must focus on meeting the needs of the students. Some of the students needed extra help because they struggled, and it causes anger because of the lack of knowledge. After some years of teaching science, Mrs. Hartley somehow ended in a similar situation as Mrs. Glades. The student reported Mrs. Hartley to the principal that she called him dumb, cursed at him, and promised to give him a failing grade. The principal called Mrs. Hartley to attend the board of education meeting. The principal explained that there would be a hearing later, and in the meanwhile, she may have to be suspended indefinitely. The principal scheduled a meeting with the parents, and the meeting was for the next day. There was a decision made to investigate the incident and suspend the teacher for an unlimited amount of time without pay. In the meanwhile, Mrs. Hartley was not allowed to work anywhere until a decision was reached. Mrs. Hartley had bills to pay, and she found two part-time jobs, and her family contributed towards her expenses. This would go on for perhaps two years before things were cleared or she was found innocent of any wrongdoing to a minor. Of course, Mrs. Hartley was not a violent teacher, nor would she verbally or physically abuse anyone.

During the hearing, the student admitted that he was not telling the truth about Mrs. Hartley. Therefore, she was set free to resume her teaching duties as a science teacher. She was also given all the back money owed to her for two years. She was offered her job back. However, she decided to seek another position in another school district. She was made to feel ashamed, and she could not face her colleagues anymore. Sometimes these challenges can cause teachers to change their profession.

CHAPTER 35

CONTROL ANGER

It was Friday, a regular school day, when two girls began talking and disagreeing with each other. Their voices began to elevate and get louder and louder. The teacher was unable to control them. When asked to dial their voices down, one of the girls responded and said, "Why don't you shut up and mind your business." Everyone in the classroom were very shocked because it was a simple discussion about the lesson. It ended in a huge heated argument, and both girls got physical, touching and pushing each other. Onlookers watched the girls and created a crowd around them. Security was called, and they arrived and took both girls to the assistant principal's office. They were reprimanded and given three days' suspension.

The parents were called to the school to discuss the reason for suspension and asked them not to return until the suspension was over, due to their inappropriate behavior. They were also instructed to write a letter of apology. After discussing the terms to the parents, one of the parents started getting angry at the assistant principal. The words, voice, and tone began to elevate, causing another misunderstanding. The AP maintained control of herself and the situation until the parent slapped her, and then the brawl began. Some of the seniors (young men) stopped them, dialed 911 due to the threats that were made towards the assistant principal and principal. One of the parent was handcuffed and taken to jail.

The challenges the teachers had to face, when one of the students returned before her suspension ended and without her parent. The student was defiant and bullying the teacher and administrators. The mother rushed to school to see what was going on. The moment she walked to the door, she was yelling loudly, "I am calling my lawyer, I am going to sue you and the board of ED." At the moment, a hearing was scheduled. The counselor would be working with the girls to help them become friends again and understand it wasn't necessary to result to violence just because someone disagreed with you.

The officer was there and walked the mother outside, talked with her, and calmed her down. The guidance counselor and the psychologist came to see why this parent was so angry and what could they do to help her.

CHAPTER 36

CULTURAL DIVERSITY

Cultural diversity is a variety of ethnic groups within the same society. Diversity is important because it helps keep the pupil's interest to want to learn the language and open the door for further knowledge. It is also important that the students are exposed to diversity, new flavor and experience because of our differences existing all over the world.

Today, many schools and districts have embraced cultural diversity, which enable the teachers to become more knowledgeable, educated, and able to use diverse language in the classroom. Teachers are then more prepared to do effective planning to educate the pupils and accepting the differences because our children learn on different levels. In that case, differentiating instructions (DI) is required and necessary so the student's needs are met. Yes, it is a challenge for the teacher today when having to prepare for state exams. The learner's needs must be addressed at all times during lesson planning and instruction. Student activities and engagement depends on effective lesson planning and delivery. However, the learners need time to digest the learning activities and delivery.

Once that has been successfully fulfilled, the teacher must begin planning for assessment to assure all needs have been met, according to state standards. Allowing children to think-pair-share, partner-talk will help with any of the shared strategies and see lifelong learning.

Having the extra support in the classroom help make the challenges today go much smoother, and the teacher is more able to address the needs of his/her pupils with calmness, peacefulness, and assurance to encourage the students to always reach higher in their practicing because that extra stretch is inside all of us. The children will surely benefit from that extra push and so will the teacher benefit from seeing the students able to demonstrate their understanding of the concept. He/she will feel pride when the pupils are able to explain their reasoning because it shows effective planning, positive delivery, and differentiated instructions, and utilizing the different strategies are important and surely a success. What a challenge!

CHAPTER 37

GENERAL AND SPECIAL EDUCATION

General and special education faces multiple challenges in an inclusion classroom. Teachers face different level of children because they are all on different grade levels. He or she must meet with each other so that they may discuss individual education program (IEP) for each child, a special needs student because there are different goals for each one of them. The teachers must come together, work cooperatively, modify lesson plans effectively, and discuss students' goals, which must reflect the lesson daily.

Pupils must get used to the new teachers by introducing himself/herself and telling them something about his/her life. Students who wish to volunteer could share. However, teachers must be the first to initiate and share. Both general education and special education teacher must establish rules and routines to maintain a safe environment that

data gathering. For the most part, assessment did not present a problem. For it was simple, teacher observation, weekly test, and standardized tests were given. But my position as a teacher in an inclusion setting calls for acquaintance with and employing a variety of assessments according to regulations governing inclusive programs for the need of my learners, and planning.

Esteban Colon's course "Assessment of Individual Differences" provided an in-depth examination of assessment. Although familiar with types, it was nice to just study assessment and important course work covered measurement and evaluation. And although assessment is an integral part of my educational duties, Mr. Colon's class provided opportunities to analyze types and rethink the appropriateness of tools I've been using to measure and evaluate student learning and also student mastery. I can honestly say that I have been better able to fine-tune remediation and develop individual study goals and lessons. Course work has also sharpened my awareness regarding the importance of assessment and also my becoming more cognizant of the possible negative uses of assessment tools.

CHAPTER 38

DIFFERENT CULTURAL COMMUNITIES

Different cultural communities can cause challenges in the classroom. Today, flexible teachers embrace their students' cultural background in the classroom, including their different languages.

The challenges today would first be the language of the students; communicating with the children and parents would be difficult because of the language barrier and misinterpretation of dialogue among the people. Clothing could be a challenge because of the children's lack of knowledge. They may tease or make fun of them, which could cause conflict in the classroom. Teachers would have to intervene and address children's differences, the language, and the clothing from different cultures. They must develop an effective lesson for the class, which will be aligned with the state's standards. A well-thought-out lesson plan must be effective for the pupils to become actively engaged and motivated, based on the children's experiences. The educator will integrate, compare, and contrast the lesson based on the children's needs, their interest, prior knowledge, their way of life, and daily activities to educate all. However, if the teacher lack knowledge of their everyday life experience of the students, the cultural background, dialects, family, and the community; the teacher must share examples from their own experiences. Lack of understanding can cause disruption for the students learning in the classroom and a serious challenge for teachers as well as students.

The support staff speaking the same language or diverse language of the students will assist the teacher and pupils to make the students welcome and apart of the class and also help with the learning process. The educator will be able to work with the pupils with peacefulness, with calmness, and with making sure each child is successful and able to complete any assigned task. Our goal is to make sure all children are learning and remain on grade level with a quality education.

English-language learners often experience great cognitive demands as they are asked to quickly learn and process both language and content in order to participate fully in daily school life. The

New York school system is, today, the largest urban educational system and is in receivership of thousands of Spanish-speaking students each school year. Depending upon the school district or other stipulation, bilingual services might not be available. As a teacher, if students are in an inclusion setting, I have come to realize that many of my charges experience much the same thing as English learners. For several years, I've instructed grades K–1 inclusion classes. Each year students prove to have difficulty with language acquisition. They have trouble with sounds and letter-word formation and often fall short of being able to construct (fully) simple sentences. These children sometimes have trouble comprehending spoken English as well as the written English language, confirming the validity of some things I have implemented in my everyday study activity.

Classroom libraries have an integral role in facilitating academic growth. English-language learners should not be intimidated by books on the library shelves. They should be presented with many opportunities during the school day to experience English in print. The library should literally "pop out at them," with large colorful illustrations appealing to their senses. Books should be chosen because their content is about those themes, children already know (families, holidays, chores, pets, friends, foods, etc.). Teachers must choose books that have few lines of simple texts. The objective is to make children pick up books and feel comfortable reading; first the pictures, and when they are capable and then the words. Library books must also be chosen to reflect the reading and comprehension levels. English-language learners exhibit books of the same theme, and topic should range from very easy to challenging. Children can move from easy reading to difficult reading and remain confident about their knowledge of the content.

A classroom library should reflect diverse genres. English-language learners need exposure to a wide range of writing styles and topics from nonfiction to poetry. Fictional stories that children identify with (such as those about their culture) that have single plots and clear language are excellent choices for the English-acquisition pupils. Content should not be filled with colloquial language or the more complex flashback sequences. Classroom teachers can also include books that present survival topics and vocabulary students need to participate everyday life, such as subjects about days of the week, time, money, or signs they might encounter on the way to school. Predictable text, which enable readers to guess the next event, helps to build students' self-confidence and sharpen their skills of predicting. Nonfiction books should be chosen for their relative illustration and simple text. These can serve as excellent support for students with diverse language abilities and levels.

Students of all levels engage and enjoy poetry. It offers students opportunities to hear the sound, and word connection and repetition of words and phrases enable learners to successfully predict what comes next. Poetry can be used to assist English-language learners with recognition option and properties of objects. Concrete or shape poem provide visual and contextual information. Concrete poems help students focus on how words are arranged, and they provide options of otherwise unfamiliar objectives.

It is extremely important that English-language learners be exposed to the spoken word during the entire school day. Read-aloud activities are great vehicle for pupils to hear and internalize sounds, words, phrases, sentences, inflections, and emotions. Read-aloud promotes fluency and comprehension. Whatever the content of genre, read-aloud engage scholars in a way that dependent-reading cannot. Learners are exposed to nuances and rhythm of

English, and hopefully, they will develop a stronger desire to practice and learn it.

Finally, teachers might wish to employ reading partnerships and hold off initiating small group reading activities in order for the English-language learners to first become brave enough to try reading in front of others. When the library has been established, it should grow. Books can be added, and others rotate. The library must never become cluttered, and another eyecatcher is to highlight new books. Children will be encouraged to read the new offerings

A well-positioned, colorful, and fully accessible classroom library is one of the most valuable tool a teacher can use to assist both inclusion students and English-language learners.

CHAPTER 39

TEACHING STRATEGIES AND IDEAS GRADES K–12

INCLUSION
Effective Teaching Strategies
Classroom Management

Strategies for Instruction
- Specify Clear Lesson Objective
- Teach to Objectives
- Make Learning Meaningful
- Prepare or Provide Important Guided Practice
- Prepare or Provide Independent Practice

Strategies for Students with Disabilities
- Sequence-Break Down the Task, Step-by-Step
- Drill-Repetition and Practice
- Daily Testing of Skills

- Segment-Breakdown Targeted Skills in Same Units
- Direct Questions-Response-Teacher Asks, Process-Related–Questions
- Control the Difficult-Task Is Sequenced from Easy to Difficult
- Technology. Use a Computer, Instructed Text Flow Charts to Facilitate Presentation and Emphasis in on Pictorial Representation.
- Group Instruction. Instruction Occurs in Small Group
- Students/Teacher Interact with the Group
- Supplement Teacher and Peer Involvement, Use Homework
- Parents, or Others, to Assist in Instruction
- Strategies for Deepening Your Effectiveness in the Classroom

Strategies for Enhancing Your Teaching
1. Get to know your students by talking with them.
2. Data tracking (Tracking data for each scholar by collecting, analyzing, recording and monitoring student's progress by using the right tools. Colleagues/Educators will use data to guide instruction. Teachers may

use classroom or your school data walls, teacher's data binders, data folders, and data clipboards for each student. This will help teachers track each pupil in their classroom).

3. Listen to your students (for example, they may ask you to read to them).
4. Ask your pupils' opinions. What can they do to improve?
5. What are your goals?
6. Keep a teacher journal (use for students' performance).
7. What are your goals during the school year?

Compare and Contrast
- Sticky Note Graph
- Think-Pair and Share
- Tic-Tac-Toe
- Form Groups
- Cubing
- Learning Contracts
- Question Choices
- Varied Text

Get Moving
- Appointment Clocks
- Four Sides Heads Together

- Jig Saw
- Literature Circle
- Reading Buddies
- Sticky Notes

Working Together
- Shared Ideas Opinions
- Learning Centers
- ShoulderShoulder
- Reading Buddies
- Tier Rubrics
- Take Notes
- KWL Charts
- Varied Organizer

High School Tips
- Scaffolding
- Reflect Response
- Anchor Activities

Classroom Management
- Set Clear Expectation and Write on Syllabus
- Tell Specific Expectation
- Be Clear About Behavioral Expectation
- Have Good Meaningful Classroom discussion

Format for Effective Lesson Planning
Date:
Grade:
Subject: (Every Subject)
Teachers' Name:
Objective:
Standards:
Essential Questions/Prior Knowledge:
Vocabulary:
Materials:
Demonstration/Model/Procedure:(whole class)
Active Involvement (whole class)
Share/Teacher Assessment:
Follow-Up/Homework:

Over-planning is fine because you can easily cut out of a plan or continue the lesson the next day.

Group A (Eagles) Group B (Dolphin)
Cluster of Six Students Cluster of Six Students Independents Students Guided Reading (Teacher)

Group C (Ravens) Group D (Lions)
Enrichment Working with Cluster of Two or Three
Partners Special Need Student
Advance Students ESL
TA Support Staff

CHAPTER 40

REFLECTION: MANY CHALLENGES

There are many challenges in the classroom! After teaching some years at the NYC Board of Education, I have had time to think and reflect about how many teachers complained, as well as myself, about being stressed, tired, and challenged in the classroom. Sometimes, teachers have said to themselves, "I can't take this stress anymore, I am leaving."

However, we were thinking about ourselves and failed to think of how Johnny and Susan may have been feeling. Teachers are not the only ones to face challenges and stress in the classroom. Look around your classroom and think about the Johnnys and the Susans you have in your class feeling the same as you do. But really, they don't know how to express their feelings in silence like we do. When pupils begin to express themselves, they begin to scream loud or hit other students. Sometimes the learners begin to display inappropriate behavior, as we always say.

At the moment, teachers see that behavior as disrespectful. But guess what, teachers? The students get frustrated and challenged too and unable to express themselves quietly. The outburst is an alarm or red flag for teachers to begin devoting extra time to investigate and see what caused such disturbing noise in the classroom. Have you ever noticed your student's facial expressions or behavior when in the early grades and unable to make simple sounds for the correct letters? Not only that, some do not know any of the alphabets, not even able to write his or her name or hold a pencil in their hand. They depend on the teacher for guidance and support. Some colleagues have forgotten the frustration and challenges our pupils may be facing in the classroom.

Of course, the child may have such unexplainable strange inner feelings. The students may be feeling inadequate, knowing they are not able to keep up with some of their peers academically. They really don't understand what's happening. So sometimes they result to screaming, hitting, kicking, and taking their peers' materials as to be their own. The frustration level may be overpowering their tiny bodies and minds, which we know it could be intolerable stress. Once knowing the cause of our underachievers' problem, teachers should make time to prepare appropriate lessons by modifying the lesson or tailor it according to the pupil's need. Consider grouping your learners. Appropriate lesson plans will minimize the level of frustration and stress for teachers as well as for the students.

Focus on their strength and weaknesses. State the objective, provide them a reason for them to listen, focus, and learn. Encourage them to be a good listener so they may become a high achiever.

1. Use flash cards.
2. Visualization.
3. Explain using simple sentences.
4. When giving direction, give simple short sentences.
5. Use picture clues.
6. Be a good motivator to capture your pupils' attention.
7. Model lessons and use chart paper with large print when introducing lessons to learners.
8. Please make sure to motivate the learners to get engaged into the lesson.
9. One way to get students engaged is by asking them questions after you (teacher) has modeled the lesson with clarity based on prior knowledge.

I have only named a few reasons why our pupils are acting inappropriately in the classroom. For example, perhaps it could be a medical issue or an unhealthy home environment, etc.

We have troubled teens who are underachievers acting out in our school system, and they are in an overcrowded classroom. Being in an overcrowded classroom can cause some students to act out because the huge class size may be overwhelming to some, and perhaps they are not in the proper setting. When students are not in the proper setting, they display inappropriate behavior because they are not getting the support that they need. Sometimes our teens may walk in the classroom late, and as soon as Johnny walked completely to the rear of the classroom, when teachers looked at the rear of the classroom, Johnny's head is usually on the desk, perhaps pretending to be fast asleep. The teacher may call on Johnny to answer a question, but he didn't respond because he didn't know the answer.

Actually, that was Johnny's way of escaping because of his learning disability. There are many Johnnys in middle school and high school having such a learning disability. To minimize inappropriate behavior, teachers must modify lessons, group students by six or seven at a table, and get support from colleagues, administration, and parental involvement.

Teachers, create a team and develop a buddy system among your colleagues. Make sure you all have meetings together once a week during your prep or after school, share ideas, and prepare lessons with modifications of the lessons for your underachievers weekly.

CHAPTER 41

JEFFREY'S SOILED SHIRT

Having a large class size is awesome, especially when you worked so hard with each child to make sure they reach grade level and some above. Their behavior was unbelievable. I would wake up in the mornings eager to meet my third-grade students. They were mostly independent workers, and they would assist the others who were not so quick to complete their class assignments.

One day, the class was divided into groups. Pupils were working so diligently to complete their projects. Suddenly, we heard such loud distasteful noises in the corridor from a child's mouth. He began to say, "I can walk, get your hands off me, woman. You are not my mother."

The security was walking Jeffrey to his class because it was his first day attending our school. She asked, "Jeffrey, please lower your voice because all students are working in their classes."

He asked, with a loud voice, "So what does that have to do with me?"

I quietly walked towards him and spoke to him with a low tone. "Jeffrey," I asked, "what is wrong?"

He responded, with a little hesitation in his voice, "I-I-I-I didn't want to come to school today because I didn't have a clean shirt and pants to wear."

"Jeffrey," I said, "the next time you have this problem, try washing your clothes yourself."

"Wow!" he said. "I didn't think of that." He asked, "What do I need to wash my clothes, other than water?"

"Perhaps a little soap detergent," I replied.

The security continued walking with Jeffrey to the classroom, and he appeared to be a little ashamed because his shirt had some food stains on it, and he was just coming directly from home wearing that food-stained shirt.

When the security reached the classroom she escorted Jeffrey inside. I spoke to him quietly and invited him into his new class, while the children were working on their projects. I asked all students for their attention so we could welcome Jeffrey and make him feel comfortable by introducing each other. My students were very friendly towards him, and Jeffrey seemed to be much calmer with less stress on his face. The students didn't pay attention to Jeffrey's stained, wrinkled shirt.

After the introduction to his peers, Jeffrey seemed to be more relaxed, and he had forgotten about his stained, wrinkled shirt. He walked around to each group and watched them work toward completion of their project.

The next day, Jeffrey came to school wearing a very colorful well-pressed shirt and matching pants. He was more relaxed, much calmer, and prepared for learning. Academically, Jeffrey was on grade level and read very well. He was engaged in class activities by asking and answering questions in complete sentences.

One day, Jeffrey noticed one of his classmates struggling try to complete her class assignment. He asked, "May I sit with Sarah so I could help her with her work?" Of course I said yes, but Sarah tried to keep it to herself.

She said, "Mrs. Carroll, I am all right." But yet she invited Jeffrey to continue to sit near her. All the other children pretended not to notice that Sarah was frustrated because of her assignment that seemed to be a little challenging.

After she was done, Jeffrey asked permission to sit in the group with Sarah. Sarah gave me a smile as to accept Jeffrey's support. I was overjoyed to see such a bright smile on her face with such approval. Of course, I permitted him to remain in that group.

Each day passed, I noticed that Sarah seemed to be more relaxed and less stressed having Jeffrey sitting near for support.

Jeffrey appeared to be more of a security blanket not only for Sarah, but for some of the others in that group.

You know, the third grade is the beginning of the testing grade for the board of education in New York City schools. To hear about test preparation, some students get very nervous and curious about what they would be facing. Many fear the unknown, which they couldn't understand what was about to happen next.

"Wow!" I said to myself, "it is really a pleasure to have Jeffrey with such compassion in my class." The learners' behavior seemed to improve each day. They became more attentive while I modeled the lessons daily. They were more engaged in the lesson by raising their hands, asking and answering questions as though they were competing with one another. The learners almost appeared to be less challenged and stress-free.

CHAPTER 42

BULLYING IN THE SCHOOLS

Teachers, have you ever had a student in your class to be very shy, trusting, dependable, and above grade level in all subjects? I once had a student named Darrell, and he was very smart, quiet, and a likable student. He went to church with his family every Sunday. He was in the choir, played the piano, and sang. He had a strong powerful-sounding voice. When he opened his mouth to sing, his voice sounded as though he was a pipe organ or instrument within him. His singing voice had mostly the entire church members standing, clapping their hands, praising the Lord with shouts of joy. Most of the girls his age were always at church to hear and see Darrell sing. He had a tremendous gift for singing. At school, Darrell would draw a lot of attention from many girls. Sometimes some of the girls would go out of their way to get Darrell's attention by throwing made-up balls of paper to get his attention and just to say hello to him. He was six feet tall, handsome, very neat-dressing student, and he loved to play basketball. He made the basketball team after practicing a lot with the coach and other team members. One day, Darrell was focusing on his studies in class. Two girls, Jayda and Candice, were in the same algebra class as Darrell. Jayda threw some paper at Darrell to get his attention; however, he saw Jayda. His interest was not Jayda, but Candice. He looked at Candice and winked his eye at her. After that, he remained focus on his class assignment. When the bell ranged, Darrell quietly and quickly went to his next class. The two girls followed him. Guess what? They were all taking the same algebra class. The two girls began to giggle as if they heard a funny joke.

The teacher invited the girls into the classroom. They sat down in the class, and Jayda again began to throw more paper at Darrell, trying to get his attention. However, still Darrell appeared not to have any interest in Jayda. After their algebra class, it was lunch time. They went into the cafeteria, got their lunch, and Darrell asked Candice to sit and have lunch with him. Candice was thrilled to know he was interested in her. She accepted his invitation. Jayda began to look at Darrell, rolling her eyes at him, she appeared to have an angry look on her face while mumbling some words under her breath. She appeared to be very envious and jealous about the two trying to develop a stronger friendship. Darrell and Candice grew up in the same community, attended the same elementary school and church every Sunday. After school, two days a week, Darrell and Candice would meet at the library and have study sessions together. The more Candice and Darrell met, the more Jayda's envy and jealousy would surface and reveal itself by speaking her mean words.

One day, Candice asked Jayda, "Why don't you join me for lunch anymore?"

Jayda replied, "Why should I meet you for lunch when you have Darrell the STD boy?"

"What did you say, Jayda?" asked Candice.

"Oh," Jayda responded, "I haven't said nothing," with that jealous tone in her voice, and she walked away. Jayda decided to develop new friends who were just as mean-spirited and spiteful as she was.

Many times, Jayda and her mean friends started following Darrell and Candice to the library. They attempted to try and disturb them while they were studying by throwing paper balls at them. They began to giggle as though they did something funny.

Darrell informed the librarian about the things Jayda and her friends were doing to them while they were trying to study. Of course, the librarian asked them to leave, and she suspended them from the library indefinitely. The girls left the library laughing with their loud voices as though they had some joke they wanted to tell.

One day, Jayda and her friends decided to start a horrible but false rumor about Darrell. First, the girls created a song. Singing out loud, "Darrell had sex with a girl. The girl smelled stinky and dirty. He went to the doctor. The doctor asked, 'Son, what have you done? I am afraid to say, you have STD!' Darrell screamed! Darrell asks, 'Doctor what can you do for me?'"

The girls continued to sing, laugh/giggle, and spread false information. The girls began making phone calls to Darrell's home, singing the song they created. Darrell wouldn't tell his parents about the unpleasant calls he received. He was ashamed even though he knew it wasn't true.

When he attended school, he began cutting some of his classes so he wouldn't be around those girls. Darrell's grades began to go down very badly. His parents were so shocked to learn about Darrell's grades. They questioned him, trying to get to the root of the problem, but he assured them it wasn't anything wrong and said, "I promise I will do better the next term." They trusted their son, so they decided to accept his answer and not question him anymore. The next day was Saturday, and Darrell was happy not to have to go to school. He stayed in his room all day doing nothing, which was unusual for him to do because on Saturdays, he usually practiced singing the songs that he would be singing at church on Sunday. Saturday was also the day that he and his father spent quality time together. Darrell pretended to be sick most of the day, so his mother gave him breakfast in his room. His parents noticed his behavior changed, but he continued to suffer in silence and not tell his parents what was troubling him. He was so ashamed, so he began to walk around with his head down and refused to face anyone.

Monday, another school day, came too soon for Darrell. He opened his phone to call his parents after arriving at school, and he noticed that someone had posted on Facebook such scandalous statement with his picture, saying "Darrell has STD". Darrell stood in the middle of the school lobby and bellowed one loud scream saying, "No! No! And he went to the floor on his knees. Many ran out of the classroom, including the guidance counselor and principal. Some of his friends ran towards him; they lifted him to his feet and walked him to the principal's office.

His best friends, said, "Man, what happened, man?"

Darrell replied in silence by throwing his phone on the principal's desk.

One of his best friends rushed to the principal's desk and grabbed the phone. His best friend opened his phone, looked at the Facebook page in complete shock, with his mouth open, but speechless for a moment. Then he said, "Mr. Thompson [the principal], you need to see this." And he moved towards the principal and handed him the phone.

The principal asked the guidance counselor, "Please call Darrell's parents, so they could take him home for remainder of the day. I will get to the bottom of this, and if anyone knows who did this, let me know, right now!" he yelled!

Darrell's parents rushed into the principal's office, and the principal privately spoke to Darrell's parents, explaining what happened to their son. They walked Darrell to the car and drove him home. His face appeared to have had the look of an innocent but humbled five-year-old boy.

Oh my God, I thought to myself, *what has that person done to that young man*. I began to think of the times when Jayda and her friends were teasing Darrell and Jayda got upset with Darrell because he didn't give her the attention she desired from him. Wow! *These girls are dangerous*, I thought to myself.

Bullying or harassment is something that no one should ever do to anyone. It is very dangerous and insensitive because of the hurt and devastation one can cause to another. At my school, there were serious consequences and actions taken against the three girls.

The next day, the principal had an assembly at school on bullying for all students and staff to attend. Every teacher had to prepare their students for participation. Mr. Thompson was given the names of the girls who were seen following Darrell daily. Darrell didn't go back to school. He was so humiliated, ashamed, and not wanting to face anyone at school, or his church friends. One Saturday morning, Darrell was found hanging from the ceiling in his room early that morning. On that early Monday morning, everyone was sad and in tears because they had heard that Darrell had committed suicide.

The principal asked their parents to come get their mean, hateful, inconsiderate, and spiteful daughters. They were expelled from the school, and they had to write a letter of apology to Darrell's parents. They began crying, saying, "We were only teasing and playing with him. It wasn't true what we said about him." All three girls were crying, saying, "I am sorry, Mr. Thompson, we didn't mean it. Please, don't make us leave the school. We won't do it anymore."

All teachers began to create and teach a lesson on bullying weekly and created individual projects. "We will not tolerate bullies here!" said Mr. Thompson. All students made posters at school in large colorful print and displayed them throughout the entire school in memory of Darrell!

CHAPTER 43

ANOTHER TYPE OF BULLYING

He was a fifth grade student with an academic score below grade level. He was not on level with his peers.

Marvin made sure to get to school late most of the time. He would walk into the classroom with his loud strong voice, saying, "good morning Mrs. Carroll and class." He began unpacking his book bag in the closet, while looking at the chalk board. He began interrupting the class by talking to himself, "I don't know how to do that!" Mrs. Carroll, he called out loud, "I need help!" I responded, "Marvin please raise your hand instead of calling out?" OK, I forgot!"

You know, Marvin not only had an academic disability. HE WAS A BULLY!

While the children are walking to the cafeteria for lunch and recess, Marvin would step on back of the children shoes, trying to make them stumble or fall on line. Marvin threaten to beat his peers up, if they didn't give him their lunch or snacks.

The children would bring their lunch from home because they didn't like the school lunch. However, Marvin didn't have that luxury, because his parents didn't have extra food for him.

Everyday the students were intimidated by Marvin and they became very frightened, to the point of crying, not wanting to go to the cafeteria. An assistant was assigned to sit with my class daily, because Marvin began to show his aggressive behavior towards the students by pushing, shoving them and using his loud voice, yelling, "I will meet you after school, watch!" He needed to be constantly corrected from the teachers and lots of praise when he completed his class assignments.

Marvin had his own way of intimidating his peers when he couldn't have his way.

Marvin was also an exceptional child. He needed an adult to monitor his behavior daily even doing play time. You know, an exceptional child is not always super smart or gifted. It has to do with a child's growth, mental and physical development.

With a child like Marvin the teacher need to bring compassion with his or her understanding of fostering a child to perform better educationally.

They need to be aware that an exceptional child is not always that who is beautiful physically, warm in behavior and average or extremely smart. The teacher needs to bring also, extreme patience in order to interact with this type of child.

Nate was as exceptional as the fifth grade student Marvin. They both required an assistant because of their needs.

Exceptional Child

You may ask yourself, what is an exceptional child? New teachers you are likely be challenged hearing this phrase, however, veteran teachers are more knowledgeable and understand about exceptional children.

Exceptional students include children that are different from the normal. For example, gifted and talented children, those that have physical attributes, a learning disability to the extent that they may need specialized education services and perhaps physical accommodation to benefit them fully.

It is important for all teachers to understand, be willing with compassion to help students with an exceptionality to make progress in the school system and perhaps for life after school.

Sometimes an exceptional child can be challenging to the teacher and also to him or herself.

My student Nate was a third grade student. He was considered and exceptional child because of his social, physical, and academic disability. He was not on the same level as his peers. His reading and writing was below grade level. Nate always had his one-on-one teacher to assist him daily. The assistant always assured that he would complete his task. An assistant with these exceptional children should use their compassion, because I realized that helps the child to bond with the teachers and classmates. Although it was challenging for him at times, Nate was motivated by his peers in the classroom.

Nates' socialization skills were very difficult. He appeared to be isolated at times. He would participate during class lessons by answering questions, even though it was challenging for him to speak. He attempted to read library books with the help of his teacher.

Teachers remember, if you have an exceptional child in your classroom, you must always modify his or her lessons. A strong relationship between a teacher and student will be built. Not only does the bond becomes stronger, it enhances the Trust.

CHAPTER 44

CYBERBULLYING

Thirty-plus years later, cyber bullying has gotten increasingly worse throughout all the school system. Intervention in the schools has been implemented by way of assembly programs, teacher's lessons, and encouraging students to create skits and poems to help minimize the behavior of others.

Cyberbullying is intimidating, threatening, and harassing messages that has caused many teenage deaths. Teenagers have been using digital devices such as phones, computers, iPad/tablets, etc. This problem isn't getting any better, because students also tease one another and think it is supposed to be alright as they say, "I was only teasing," laughing with a loud voice. Again, they say it was really a joke, "Can't you take a joke?"

However, these messages are not jokes. These are cruel messages that leave pupils with the feelings of hopelessness and then lead to serious consequences to the victim. After all, the teasing and insulting messages can cause irreversible damage and tragedy, which causes police investigations. Many cyberbullying also consist of threats, provocative insults, racial ethnic slurs. There are times many teens engage in gay bashing, which has been rising limitless, causing unbelievable crimes. They are quick to say, "I am sorry, I didn't mean it." However, it doesn't change the damage or hurt that it has caused.

When students or adults experience such cruel types of behavior, it is unacceptable to walk away from these horrible crimes. When at school, the principal, guidance counselor, parents, and security officers should be informed immediately before any disaster reaches a point of no return. In the chapter about Darrell, he was too ashamed to tell anyone. He thought he could handle it alone and not burden anyone, so when Darrell slipped into such dark place, he then realized that he wasn't strong mentally to speak out in time for support. He waited too long because there was complete darkness surrounding him. In the future, I hope to obtain more information to enhance my knowledge and experience in the classroom on cyberbullying.

ABOUT THE AUTHOR

Elizabeth Scott Carroll is a teacher. She works collaboratively with her colleagues by team planning and strategizing to assure that all pupils are successful in their subjects.

She walks with boldness and confidence of assurance with the preparation of lessons for the day. She shows ownership of her classroom by meeting and greeting each student daily as they enter the classroom. A checklist is also used to determine each child's attendance.

She has a warm spirit, compassion of love for her teaching and students, and the love and kindness among all scholars.

Elizabeth has high expectations, maximize instructional time, monitors her pupils' learning. She caters to their comprehension and reflects on their craft.

Active involvement is another one of her strategies to keep them engaged, make them a part of the lesson taught by asking and answering questions. She knows when to listen and show clarity of lessons taught with a positive attitude. Sometimes she brings a little humor to make them laugh when she feels that it is necessary.

Parental involvement is very important to her. Elizabeth works collaboratively with her parents and makes sure her students achieve even if she has to modify her lessons so they may have a better understanding.

There are lots of challenges in the classroom, not just the scholars, but teachers also develop that feeling of stress. Elizabeth Scott Carroll embraces the challenges and changes with a positive attitude. She circulates through her classroom with grace so the pupils could feel her presence to avoid the stress that may arise. She uses the buddy system, parental involvement, team planning, scholars sitting in groups of six so they may be supportive of one another.